BFI Modern Classics

Rob White
Series Editor

Advancing into its second ⸺ ⸺ w a mature art form
with an established list of cl⸺ ⸺porary cinema is so subject
to every shift in fashion regard⸺ ⸺cs, morals and ideas that
judgments on the true worth of ⸺ ⸺t films are liable to be risky and
controversial; yet they are essential if we want to know where the cinema
is going and what it can achieve.

As part of the British Film Institute's commitment to the promotion
and evaluation of contemporary cinema, and in conjunction with the
influential BFI Film Classics series, BFI Modern Classics is a series of
books devoted to individual films of recent years. Distinguished film
critics, scholars and novelists explore the production and reception of
their chosen films in the context of an argument about the film's
importance. Insightful, considered, often impassioned, these elegant,
beautifully illustrated books will set the agenda for debates about what
matters in modern cinema.

The Wings of the Dove

Henry James in the 1990s

Robin Wood

bfi Publishing

First published in 1999 by the
British Film Institute
21 Stephen Street, London W1P 2LN

The British Film Institute is the UK national
agency with responsibility for encouraging
the arts of film and television and conserving
them in the national interest.

Series design by Andrew Barron &
Collis Clements Associates

Picture editing by Liz Heasman

Typeset in Italian Garamond and Swiss 721BT
by D R Bungay Associates, Burghfield, Berks

Printed in Great Britain by
Norwich Colour Print, Drayton, Norfolk

British Library Cataloguing-in-Publication Data
A catalogue record for this book is available
from the British Library
ISBN 0-85170-734-3

Contents

Preface: The Problem of Literary Adaptation

The Christmas before last (1997) I gave my son and his wife (on the strength of its enthusiastic critical reception) the six videos of the 1995 BBC adaptation of *Pride and Prejudice*, and we decided to watch an episode a week together on Sunday evenings. I believe we tried quite hard to interest ourselves in the first two episodes; the unconcealed yawns began around episode three. We struggled on to the end, where the tedium was perceptibly lessened by the sudden appearance of Barbara Leigh-Hunt as Lady Catherine de Bourgh. (A friend who admires the series informed me later that Leigh-Hunt was the one serious blot on the otherwise 'faithful' production.)

The following week I showed a video of the 1940 MGM version of Jane Austen's marvellous novel, and we were all, more or less, captivated (I somewhat less). It is not a very good film but at least it is *alive*, partly because Mary Boland gives such a wonderful performance, not as Mrs Bennett, but as Mary Boland. If her (not Jane Austen's) Mrs Bennett is a far lesser assumption than her Effie Floud in *Ruggles of Red Gap*, this is partly because the film is not directed by Leo McCarey but by Robert Z. (for Zilch) Leonard, but much more because there remained in 1940, and still lingers today, some ancient myth that the adaptation of a great novel has to be 'faithful'. (McCarey would have rewritten the whole screenplay, with the co-operation of his actors, and there would certainly have been a scene in which Mr Darcy lost his trousers, quite possibly pulled off by Ms Boland. It would have been a great movie.)

I want, then, to begin with a simple statement, the truth of which is seldom acknowledged: literature is literature, film is film. It's really as simple as that. There is no such thing as a faithful adaptation. When people talk about faithful adaptations they usually seem to mean that the film follows the plot of the novel. This represents a profound (if doubtless well-intentioned) insult to great literature, the greatness of which resides in the writer's grasp of the potentialities of language – movement from word to word, sentence to sentence, paragraph to paragraph – which cannot in any way be reproduced in film. To reduce a great novel to its plot is merely to reveal a total incapacity for reading it. But the notion of the faithful adaptation is equally insulting to film. It implies that film is the inferior art, and should be content (or even proud) to reproduce precisely what it can never hope to reproduce: the movement of the author's words on paper. The film-maker has every right to take what s/he wants from a novel (be it Mickey Spillane or Tolstoy), and make of it whatever suits her or his interests. That is why Cuaron's *Great Expectations* is (at the lowest estimate) a far more *interesting* film than David Lean's, which is mere (attempted) reproduction.

I consider myself as great an admirer of Henry James as anyone else in the world, and (with major reservations) I love his novel *The Wings of the Dove*. I shall, in what follows, relate the recent film version to its source, but I shall also treat it as a *film*, a work of art in its own right, not as some misguided (and failed) attempt at producing a replica.

The Wings of the Dove: Henry James in the 1990s

Henry James and the Feminist Melodrama

Lovers of James's fiction may be surprised, and even outraged, by the association of his name with the term 'melodrama', so I had better concede immediately that (except in certain of the early novels and stories, most obviously *The American*) James is the least 'melodramatic' of writers. The term evokes qualities such as excess, overt emotionalism, exaggeration, 'in-your-face-ness', and James in his mature work is characteristically the subtlest, most reticent, most indirect of writers, leaving – for all the ever-increasing stylistic elaboration – so much to be inferred or intuited, read between the lines. Yet if one reduces the novels to their plots (of course a monstrous reduction) they can be seen to relate in a number of cases to the thematic concerns of what we have come to call the Hollywood 'woman's picture' that finds its most powerful and frequent generic form in melodrama. Novel after novel, tale after tale, reveals itself as centrally preoccupied with the position of women in a patriarchal culture, their oppression and subordination, their manipulation by men, the male drive to control and possess them, the women's resistance and (occasional) transgression of the patriarchal laws. His heroines, even when defeated, reveal in their evolution ever deeper resources of strength.

It could be argued, I think, that melodrama is a form of expression to which the cinema lends itself with particular ease. Literature has its own potentials for excess, but they can hardly compete with the potentials inherent in the huge close-up, jagged (hysterical) editing, violent colour schemes, passionate music. Such potentials (for such is the complexity of cinema) can be used in radically different ways, for the direct expression of emotional extremes as in the melodramas of King Vidor (*Duel in the Sun*, *Ruby Gentry*, *Beyond the Forest*) or ironically as in Sirk (*There's Always Tomorrow*, *Imitation of Life*). Or there is the possibility of a deliberate, perverse reversal of stylistic expectations, as in the remarkable anti-melodramatic melodramas of Preminger in the 40s and 50s. What could be more melodramatic in content than the final moments of *Angel Face*? Yet what could be *less* melodramatic than Preminger's rigorous (and non-judgmental) refusal of melodramatic effect, with minimal editing and everything in long shot?

It is perhaps their underlying melodramatic potential that has attracted film-makers to James's novels and stories. I shall argue later (and readers may take this as a 'trailer' or, as it is called in North America, a preview) that the particular distinction of *The Wings of the Dove* lies in its respect for the novel's melodramatic basis combined with the ability to find cinematic equivalents for something of James's subtlety, complexity and ambiguity.

James in the 90s:
Washington Square and *The Portrait of a Lady*

Is it coincidence that the three recent film adaptations of James novels – *Washington Square*, *The Portrait of a Lady* and *The Wings of the Dove* – are all, essentially, feminist melodramas, and that all three share the same basic premise? In all three a young, innocent American heiress falls prey to the attractions and persuasions of a suitor, in whose sincerity she believes completely but who is really after her money, the narrative reaching its climax and, subsequently, its resolution in response to her discovery of his true motive. They are in fact three of the only four James novels with this premise (the fourth, *The Golden Bowl*, has been the subject of a recent BBC adaptation). One might suggest, tentatively, that the first great wave of feminism (the suffragette movement) nurtured the novels, at least on an unconscious level (the conscious one being sadly represented by *The Bostonians*). The second wave, the far more sweeping and comprehensive radical feminism of the 60s and 70s, and the heightened awareness of women's oppression and exploitation that it produced, was a potent influence on the films. Certainly, the implicit feminism of the novels is rendered explicit, especially in the two films directed by women, *Washington Square* and *The Portrait of a Lady*.

If the three novels – and *The Golden Bowl* – are variations on a premise, it must be stressed that, given their shared basis, they could scarcely be more different from one another. Their heroines are quite distinct in personality, degree of intelligence and awareness, and personal situation; the suitors range from the insidiously seductive and hateful Gilbert Osmond of *The Portrait of a Lady* to the wholly sympathetic Merton Densher of *The Wings of the Dove,* whose only fault is completely understandable (in the context) human weakness. Of the three, *The Portrait of a Lady* comes closest to acknowledging an explicit feminist intention, especially in its conclusion, which one might reasonably describe as 'lesbian' in the wider sense made accessible by the women's movement: female bonding, for mutual support against male domination. Henrietta Stackpole (whom it is tempting to read as lesbian in the narrower sense) marries an ineffectual adorer for whom she feels nothing beyond a sort of affectionate contempt solely in order to remain in Europe, and her motivation for remaining in Europe (of which, as a chauvinistic American, she is extremely critical) is solely to be accessible to Isabel. Isabel, in her turn, decides to go back to a wretched and loveless marriage and an intolerable domestic situation solely to attempt to rescue Pansy Osmond from the machinations of her loathsome father. The bonds of commitment among the three women represent the novel's ultimate 'positive', illuminating its otherwise dark conclusion. I find it inexplicable that Jane Campion, despite her clear feminist position, makes nothing of this: Henrietta disappears from the narrative, and Campion withholds any information as to Isabel's final intentions.

Perhaps of all James's novels, *Washington Square* offers itself most readily for appropriation as feminist melodrama – and, for that matter, for translation into film, being relatively short and compact, lacking the scope, structural complexity, and multiple characters of *The Portrait of a Lady*. But, while both adaptations translate James into melodrama, they do so in somewhat different ways. Holland unashamedly embraces the 'melodramatic' style, with its directness and excess: even the most extreme instances (the teenage Catherine losing control of her bladder when expected to recite a poem at her father's birthday party – a moment that suggests we are being given a remake of *The Exorcist* – and Catherine's hysterical pursuit of Morris through the streets during a downpour, culminating in her fall in the mud) are not really out of place within the overall context, however those who demand fidelity may shudder. *The Portrait of a Lady* (the novel), three times as long, far more elaborate, and far more concerned with its heroine's inner life, the analysis of a consciousness, presents greater challenges for the film-maker, which Campion attempts to meet by simplifying and coarsening the leading characters (though whether she was aware of that is uncertain, as it is a direct consequence of the casting).

It was inevitable that Agnieszka Holland's film would be compared (generally unfavourably) to *The Heiress*; it seems to me that the comparison usefully illuminates Holland's achievement, highlighting *Washington Square*'s far greater detail, density and complexity. Doubtless its superiority is due in great part to the fact that it was adapted directly from James's novel, where Wyler's much more celebrated film was drawn from an already greatly simplified (and melodramatised) play. Wyler's task was to fill out a somewhat thin and schematic scenario by means of his actors' performances (Ralph Richardson, especially, restoring much of the complexity of James's original). Holland's task was to pare down a short but dense and subtle novel to the scope of a hundred minute film, preserving the density and subtlety as far as possible while using it also as a vehicle for her own preoccupations.

In one respect she actually improves on James, adding a tragic dimension the novel lacks. Dr Sloper's treatment of his daughter is unforgivable (though James makes it entirely understandable), yet he is clearly right about Morris Townsend – Catherine's marriage would be disastrous for her, she would be first exploited then neglected. But by depriving his heroine of even the possibility of happiness James makes her 'case' merely hopeless. The problem is carried over, unresolved and apparently unrecognised, into *The Heiress*, where Montgomery Clift is allowed or encouraged to play Morris as a two-dimensional, shallow schemer endowed with insidious charm and plausibility. When, at the end of the film, we are suddenly asked to believe that he now wants Catherine's love as well as her money, this comes across as perfunctory and unconvincing, a cheap attempt at a final ironic twist. (In James he returns as he left, except that he is now coarse and unattractive, deprived by failure of his spurious charm.)

Holland seems quite aware of this problem (though her solution may be felt to create new ones): she makes it clear that, as Catherine blossoms, Morris begins to respond. This is not spelt out, but it is very clear in the acting: watch Ben Chaplin during the central, and crucial, confrontation with Albert Finney, and it is impossible to doubt his sincerity. He still, of course, requires Catherine's inheritance, he is not suddenly transformed from a self-serving opportunist into a spellbound Romeo. But his newly-developed feeling for Catherine as a person is evident, and the suggestion is that, given sufficient wealth to satisfy his extravagant ambitions for a future of comfort and idleness, he could have made Catherine happy. While almost any means of escape from her father would be an improvement, neither James's novel nor *The Heiress* holds out even that much hope. The problem is that this transfers all the opprobrium the reader/viewer is made to feel from Townsend to Dr Sloper, whose inability to see that he is *not* acting for his daughter's good turns him into a kind of monster.

Equally intelligent – given her feminist commitment – is Holland's transformation (or extension?) of James's ending. *The Heiress* opted for a melodramatic pessimism: with the (ambiguously) reformed Morris Townsend beating hysterically on her door, Catherine takes her lamp and mounts the stairs to her room – the room where, metaphorically at least, it is implied that she will spend the rest of her life, in solitude and bitterness. James leaves her relatively tranquil – firm, but rational and controlled. Holland, without surrendering to any temptation to a sentimentalist's happy ending, allows her to find a certain modest satisfaction as a kind of one-woman daycare centre for young children. If not exactly fulfilled she is at least content, and the experiences of Catherine's own childhood, a childhood without respect, will permit her to be a beneficent influence.

While *Washington Square* is clearly the more successful of the two films, *The Portrait of a Lady* (which has far greater problems of adaptation to overcome) is in some ways the more interesting. Campion's work never lacks distinctness and a certain distinction, the distinction of a film-maker in love with her chosen medium: *The Portrait of a Lady* is consistently intelligent and sensitive in its use of colour (the images become systematically depleted as the narrative unfolds, from the verdure and sunshine of the opening through the progressively sombre Italian sequences to the barren, snowbound conclusion), widescreen composition and camera placement, and one can derive considerable pleasure from the film by concentrating on the *mise-en-scène*.

Its basic problem is the one endemic to literary adaptations: its hesitation between 'faithful' and 'free' (one might compare Cuaron's splendid *Great Expectations*, where the adaptation is so free that, after a while, one ceases to think of Dickens at all). Its most obvious liberties can be easily discounted: mere annoyances that could be cut from the film without the slightest loss to narrative coherence or thematic sense. There are three: the absurd and irrelevant credit sequence in which various young women in modern dress disport themselves or strike poses amid trees, as if auditioning for modelling jobs somewhere between GAP and Ralph Lauren; the fantasy sequence (as jarring in the film as its equivalent would have been in the novel) in which Isabel imagines herself erotically caressed on a bed by Ralph Touchett, Lord Warburton and Casper Goodwood simultaneously (is she trying to choose or wondering whether she could perhaps juggle all three?); and the parodic sequence, presented as an old black-and-white movie in academy ratio, that fills in the period of Isabel's travels while she considers Osmond's proposal and decides that she loves him.

The problem goes deeper: the film, obvious aberrations apart, continuously presents itself as a representation of the novel, yet could not possibly satisfy anyone who loves and admires it. I have already mentioned the casting. Nicole Kidman works very hard and clearly takes her role very seriously (one feels, watching her, that one is studying the *mechanics* of acting, although there is little about the film one could call Brechtian), but she is many miles short of James's Isabel: beautiful, vibrant, longing fully to experience life in all its complexity, with an intelligence fatally flawed by the innocence that permits her to take

Osmond at face value. Who could have undertaken this role successfully? I can think of no one available today; perhaps Jean Simmons or Jennifer Jones when they were in their twenties. Today, perhaps, we should be thankful that at least we were not given Parker Posey (though she would have given Osmond his comeuppance pretty briskly). But James's Isabel captivated three men and was viewed by a fourth as a perfect *objet d'art* for his collection and self-enhancement. Kidman's Isabel comes across as a somewhat ordinary young woman with no remarkable qualities; the actress's persona (perfectly suited to her role in *To Die For*) is far too 'knowing' for her to be capable of embodying Isabel's innocence, without which her capitulation to (and misreading of) Osmond cannot be convincing; worst of all, she is not likely to be capable of empathising with the predicament of Pansy Osmond, or of sacrificing her possible future to save her.

Then there is the casting of John Malkovich, who plays Osmond as a transparent sleazeball, whom only a complete idiot could fail to identify instantly as such. This thoroughly undermines James's conception, but it might have been made to work on a lower level: unintelligent, easily duped young woman with money falls for cultured dilettante after her wealth and lives to regret it. This would result in a *simple* melodrama, culminating logically either in him murdering her or her murdering him. But Campion's aspirations forbid descent to such freedoms: her loyalty to James compels her to make it clear that Osmond does not marry Isabel *solely* for her money, he wants her as an exquisite possession, converting a vibrant woman into the *portrait* of a lady to adorn his salon and show off to his admiring guests. But that is a role that Kidman's Isabel, a small personality lacking depth and nuance, is patently unequipped to fill.

James: The Late Period

The beginning of James's 'late' period, in which *The Wings of the Dove* occupies a prominent position as one of the major (if flawed) achievements, can be dated fairly precisely. It follows the ten-year period in which he all but abandoned the writing of novels in a determined but disastrous attempt to establish himself as a dramatist in the London theatre. *The Turn of the Screw*, *What Maisie Knew* and *The Awkward Age* are already stylistically distinct from the earlier works (though still of course recognisable as products of the same subtle, complex and fastidious mind). None of James's novels could conceivably be described as 'easy reading', but his demands on the reader increase appreciably here. Sentences are more and more elaborate, every statement immediately qualified by a proliferation of subordinate clauses, the 'action' increasingly internalised in the consciousness of the characters, whose motivations become increasingly ambiguous. The process is highly but not quite fully developed in *The Wings of the Dove*; its culmination is reached in James's final major novel, *The Golden Bowl*, and I want to turn to that extraordinary work first in order to define the problems these novels produce, for the reader but even more for the courageous, foolhardy would-be adapter.

There are two justifications for offering at least a perfunctory account of *The Golden Bowl* here before examining in greater detail *The Wings of the Dove* (the novel and the film). First, the two novels are intricately linked, be it as variations on a theme or as two different games played with the same counters: a pair of impoverished lovers, and the American heiress the man reluctantly courts (*The Wings of the Dove*) or marries (*The Golden Bowl*) for her money. James's evolution can be seen partly in the increasingly complex and ambivalent attitude to his American characters and their relationship to Europe and Europeans. In the early novel *The American* (his closest work to what we think of as 'melodrama') the innocence of the significantly named Christopher Newman (a Columbus rediscovering Europe from the New World) is never called into question, even though the treatment is intermittently satirical: he is simply what he seems, and the novel confronts him with Europeans whose deviousness and corruption are also unquestioned. In the late books such certitude and confidence can no longer exist. The Europeanised protagonist of the remarkable late short story *The Jolly Corner* returns to America to confront (in the form of the grotesque phantom he discovers haunting his old home) the crude, corrupt and vulgar monster he would have become had he stayed there. In *The Ambassadors*, Strether visits

Europe to retrieve the recalcitrant young prodigal Chad for his predestined New England heritage, and ends up advising him to stay in France. Milly Theale (but not Maggie Verver) is the exception to this general reversal, but she is presented as a very special case, very young, totally sheltered, and dying of an incurable illness. Even there, we may tentatively ascribe James's failure to 'realise' her more intimately to his fear that, had he probed deeper, she might prove to be a Maggie Verver after all.

The second justification is the more important: *The Golden Bowl* marks the culmination of a continuum of investigation/exploration, at once aesthetic, moral and psychological, that effectively began with *What Maisie Knew* and *The Awkward Age*, but of which *The Wings of the Dove* is the most evolved and ambitious prior production. To look back at it from *The Golden Bowl* is to see very clearly the direction in which James was heading, to arrive at a point where all clarity (of motivation, perception, moral judgment) is no longer possible, and where all certitude dissolves. *The Golden Bowl* contains one character (spectator, commentator, occasional participant) who continues to believe that human behaviour can be understood and defined, despite the fact that all the book's evidence indicates the opposite: Fanny Assingham, wife of a phlegmatic British colonel. Ironically, it is Fanny who is given some of the book's key statements: 'Ah, who can say what passes between people in such a relationship?' (p.417, Penguin edition); and, on the next page: 'There are many things', said Mrs Assingham, 'that we shall never know.'

F. R. Leavis notoriously attacked late James, reacting against the then general consensus that the late novels represent 'the major phase'. In so far as he was rectifying a severe critical imbalance, the attack was salutary: I see no reason whatever to maintain that *The Golden Bowl* is a greater novel than *The Portrait of a Lady*. It is, however, a very different one, and the difference was not of a kind with which Leavis was fully equipped to cope. His constant preoccupation (which tended toward the exclusive) was with moral values, moral perceptions, moral judgments. His preoccupation, it must be said, has been grotesquely simplified by his enemies, since it was never tied to a preconceived, 'given', conventional morality but guided always by a concern for 'life'. It was at once his greatest strength and his chief limitation. It made Leavis a great critic, but it left him ill-equipped to cope adequately with 'modernist' novels whose content and tone are pervasively influenced by the Freudian discovery of the unconscious. For what becomes of the status of a moral judgment, or even of a clear moral perception, of the characters' actions and choices, when those actions and choices are revealed as ultimately determined by motivations beyond their conscious control? It is this limitation that prevents Leavis from doing full justice to *The Wings of the Dove* (though his brief account of it is not exactly unjust), and leads to his disastrous misreading (as it seems to me) of *The Golden Bowl*.

The four leading characters of *The Golden Bowl* are not 'complex' in the traditional novelistic sense, i.e. many-sided, contradictory, etc. Isabel Archer is a far more complex character in that sense than her late counterpart Maggie Verver. James, in his final phase, passed beyond the construction of complex characters to the far harder and more dangerous task of attempting to define the complexities of the human mind: the movement of thought, the problem of trying to 'read' others within a context of 'civilised' mores in which nothing can be expressed openly or directly, the hazards (perhaps the illusion) of perception, the labyrinths of motivation, the intricate ways in which a decision is reached. This is what distinguishes the late novels from the early novels. *The Portrait of a Lady* is still firmly grounded in the nineteenth century: however complex the characters, James presumes to know them, and to communicate his knowledge of them to the reader; by *The Golden Bowl* (and via *The Wings of the Dove*) all confidence in such an undertaking has dissolved beyond the possibility of restoration. This partly accounts for the nature of the (celebrated or infamous) 'late' style, with its convolutions, its endless qualifications, its apparent tautologies which in fact are the manifestation of his groping for an ever greater precision but which tend often to increase the reader's sense of uncertainty and confusion. But there was another, more prosaic factor which facilitated James's evolution into a demonstrably twentieth century novelist: in his later years he discovered the benefits of the typewriter and the stenographer. The late novels were all dictated; the characters' efforts to understand themselves and each other were paralleled by their author's struggle to find the right phrase, the right metaphor, the most exact formulation, to define the actual movement of consciousness. To read *The Golden Bowl* is to 'hear' him writing aloud.

There seems to be no evidence that James ever read Freud, though he could scarcely, during the first decade of the twentieth century, not have heard about his theories; if not, then we must postulate a parallel development, something 'in the air' at the time. Freud himself insisted that he didn't 'discover' the unconscious, that it had already been discovered (though not mapped out) in the works of the great artists. Indeed, we can find passages in *Emma* that reveal a very clear awareness that our conscious perceptions often depend on insights or impulses below the level of consciousness.

The characters of *The Golden Bowl* are constantly struggling to understand what they can confidently know about each other, and what the others know about their knowledge: for example, when Maggie grasps that her husband and her best friend (who is also her father's wife, hence her stepmother, though roughly the same age) are involved in a passionate love affair – since when? how far has it gone? how serious is it? – her concern is to make out whether Amerigo, Charlotte and her father know that *she* knows (James's image is of her plucking 'the small wild blossoms of her dim forest'). The characters are groping – as is their author – in a world of shadows and elusive half-lights, of perceptions that may be misperceptions, for a certainty that is always out of reach. This is why it is one of the most difficult books in the language to *read* (in both the literal and figurative senses): we grope for James's meaning as he gropes for an understanding of his own creations who, in their turn, are groping for an understanding of each other. Crucial to this shadow world is James's awareness that his characters never entirely understand themselves or their own motivations: the sense that their actions and behaviour are governed by impulses for which they constantly seek a rationale but which lie far below the control of their conscious minds. The characters are at once agonisingly *self*-conscious and dangerously *un*conscious of their true motivations – an unconsciousness that sets them free to do things they couldn't possibly do consciously. What one witnesses in the late novels is no less than the dissolution of the nineteenth century view of character as something integrated and definable. This is one of many reasons why there can never again be another *Middlemarch* or *Little Dorrit*.

It is in the late novels, and only in them, that the last traces of melodrama disappear from James's work: they still hover in the distant background of *The Wings of the Dove*, but are entirely absent from *The Golden Bowl*. Osmond and Madame Merle, however complex and subtly drawn, are basically 'melodramatic' villains because they both know perfectly well what they are doing and why. The ultimate tragic irony of *The Golden Bowl* is that it is the 'pure', 'innocent' Maggie Verver, James's final incarnation of the 'American princess', who is gradually revealed as the book's arch-manipulator, whose manipulations bring about disaster. It is Maggie who initially manipulates her father into marrying Charlotte, and it is she who finally manipulates him into taking Charlotte back to America, thereby producing two loveless and desolate marriages, complementary prisons on either side of the Atlantic. Yet James can continue, to the end, reasonably to insist upon Maggie's 'innocence'. It is a very precarious innocence, built upon a suppression of self-knowledge which, we are often made to feel, forces itself at times perilously close to the surface of consciousness: a terrible and terrifying innocence.

Leavis appears to have taken the innocence at face value; for him, the novel's failure lies in its sentimental idealisation of Maggie and her father and what he sees as their final triumph, presented apparently without irony. This is clearly not the place for a detailed analysis of the whole novel (in any case a daunting undertaking); an examination of its final paragraph must suffice. If we are in any doubt as to the exact force of Amerigo's 'I see nothing but you', doesn't the immediate context clarify it beyond a doubt? Amerigo *'tried'* – and 'all too clearly' – 'to please her'. The truth of his assertion 'so strangely lighted his eyes' that Maggie suddenly can't meet their intensity. She 'buried her own in his breast' not out of triumph or ecstasy but 'as for pity and terror of them'. This scarcely conveys the sense of some ideal marital union. The 'golden bowl' will always have its flaw, perhaps because it is an artificial construct that, as a *false* symbol of utopian perfection in relationships, cannot take into account the complexities of human desire and their impossibility of fulfilment within an ideology which is rooted in money, hence centred on principles of ownership which encourage the buying of human beings as well as antiques.

From Novel to Film

The Wings of the Dove occupies in James's development a mid position between *The Awkward Age* and *The Golden Bowl* – the former, among the least read and most perplexing of James's novels, consisting predominantly of often elliptical dialogue, the fruit and validation of his apparently wasted years writing unproducible plays; the latter predominantly devoted to analysing the movement of the characters' consciousness, with a continuous awareness of how that movement is determined by the Freudian unconscious. One wonders how many people (unless retired, like myself), in this age of breathless rush characterised by a rapidly diminishing attention span, find the time or the patience to read James's late novels: it took me a full month to re-read *The Golden Bowl* in preparation for this monograph, going over and over the convoluted sentences, then back over the paragraph that contains them, in a not always successful attempt to confidently grasp all the implications. I was consequently somewhat bemused (or, more cynically, amused) by the efforts of all the journalist critics I read on the film version of *The Wings of the Dove* to establish (at least by implication) their intimate familiarity with the novel. The favourite ploy was to remark knowingly that of course James would never have written the explicit sex scenes (a safe enough guess). None in my experience mentioned that, for example, the Venice section that takes up less than a quarter of the novel occupies more than half the film, or that the novel contains no nocturnal gondola ride, no carnival night, and no climbs up scaffolding in semi-restored churches. No one, in fact, saw fit to point out that not one single scene in the film has a close counterpart in the novel (the closest is in fact the climactic scene between Kate and Merton, though in James they keep their clothes on).

Hossein Amini's screenplay is indeed a remarkable achievement. You would have to know and love the novel very intimately to be capable of so complete a transformation of its surface while, at the same time, preserving its essentials with such sensitivity and intelligence. There is no attempt to do the impossible – capture the inner flow of thought and perception (James's central preoccupation), in, for example, extended voiceovers accompanying and explicating close-ups of people thinking. Instead, everything has been fully dramatised – or, better, *cinematised* – with objective correlatives found, wherever possible, for internal states. The result is a triumphant paradox: the experience of 'reading' the film is totally different from that of reading the novel, yet one almost (I have some reservations) never feels that James has been betrayed. Here for once is an adaptation at once completely 'free' yet faithful to the novel's essence.

That said, it remains important to examine the major instances where the film diverges from the book: not its 'scenes', which are without exception quite different, but significant alterations in narrative and character. The question to be asked is not 'Are these betrayals of a "classic" original?' But 'Do the changes benefit or weaken the film?'

1. The film dispenses with Kate's sister Marian. It is crucial to both novel and film that Kate, despite the fact that she manipulates both her lover and her best friend in her ultimately disastrous (for all three) plot to obtain access to Milly's money, be established as intensely sympathetic and remain so throughout. If she becomes merely a scheming villainess the tragic structure (it is above all *her* tragedy) collapses. Marian, doubtless, was found redundant. Clearly in reducing a 400-page novel to a film of manageable length something has to go, and James himself seems largely to forget about her: after her early prominence she is barely mentioned until near the end. She is, however, of some importance in intensifying our sense of the intolerable pressures on Kate. Marian is widowed, with four young children and no career (she has never aspired beyond marriage), she is as dependent upon Kate's access to wealth as is their father. Kate is presented as the only intelligent and responsible surviving member of the family, with father

and sister shamelessly dependent upon her strength and fidelity, and she has already (before the beginning of the novel) turned over to Marian half her share of the meagre income (two hundred pounds a year) left the sisters by their mother. Removing Marian from the narrative inevitably tends to weaken our sense of Kate's desperation, throwing more weight on her *personal* need. However, the film finds ways – direct and indirect – to compensate partly for this.

2. The direct way is to make Kate's father (Michael Gambon, pathetic and repulsive in roughly equal measures) even more hopelessly lost, sunk and helpless than he is in the book. James offers him as a seedy failure with a vaguely disreputable background (we are never told exactly what he has done or how far he has sunk, James being notoriously reticent about sordid detail). The film converts the vagueness into the explicitness and excess of melodrama: he is a drunkard and an opium addict, a hopelessly lost soul who has simply given up. Yet he is Kate's father, and the revelation that Aunt Maud is paying him off to leave Kate alone increases her humiliating sense of dependency on Maud.

   The film also uses the father – together with Kate's continuing emotional attachment to the dead mother, whose grave we see her cleaning – to emphasise the necessity of money, within a culture dominated by it, for successful human relationships. The film makes the point more explicitly than it is made in the novel: without money, a life with Merton Densher might well repeat the disintegration and misery of her parents' marriage. The assumption, common to James's late books, that, within a capitalist culture, love, however 'true', is unlikely to survive extreme poverty is (if prosaic and anti-romantic) perfectly realistic.

3. I am far from sure that the film is helped by its attempt (at least in its early stages) to present Merton Densher as a political radical. If it was intended as a way of making manifest the radical implications of James's work, it seems far too crude and simplistic. It also creates a problem the film fails to resolve: Merton, in the pub scene near the beginning and in the office scene later, when he explains to Kate his

exposé of the medical profession's mercenary exploitation of prostitutes, seems so convincingly committed that his abrupt declaration, in Venice, that he didn't really care all that much comes as a betrayal of the character the film has established. James's Densher wrote nothing more inflammatory than a 'literary' column about the countries and cities he visited, his principles amounting to no more than an apolitical refusal to be 'vulgar'. James has him meditate on his 'private inability' ever to make money, in an environment increasingly demanding the sensational or titillating. The film's Densher shows every possibility of becoming, if not a millionaire, at least a highly successful journalist, forceful and outspoken. The essential passivity of James's Densher makes his capitulation to Kate's manipulations more plausible.

4. A potential problem – one of possible confusion – arises from the film's depiction of the sexual relations between Kate and Merton. James, without ever becoming explicit, subtly conveys a convincing erotic charge. It is clear, however, that the relationship has not been consummated – indeed, James is quite explicit about this: 'She could say to herself that from that hour they had kept company; that had come to represent, technically speaking, the range and limit of their tie' (p. 40 – all references are to the Penguin edition). The basis of this is no doubt the very different sexual mores of Victorian/Edwardian times that stressed the 'purity' of women before marriage (difficult, perhaps, for today's audience to comprehend, or at least to believe that it was paid more than lip service), but also the fear of discovery. Kate could not risk being seen entering Merton's apartment, and she is living with Aunt Maud (who disapproves of the relationship, having her own plans for Kate). This gives great force to Merton's virtual blackmail of Kate in Venice, to which only extreme sexual desperation could drive so scrupulous a young man to descend: he will agree to her scheme to encourage Milly's growing attraction if Kate will give herself to him. This force is largely lost in the film, although if we read it carefully the case is no different. Here, the couple appear to have been engaged in a passionate erotic relationship since before the start: the film opens with

their chance meeting on the London Underground after a period of presumably total abstinence since the death of Kate's mother and her adoption (with strings attached) by her aunt. Their irresistible mutual attraction provokes a highly charged and reckless erotic encounter in an elevator. Later, Kate has no qualms about visiting Merton's apartment and spreading herself provocatively on his bed. The film in fact makes it clear that this is the first time she has been there and that intercourse does not take place, but the viewer has every excuse for feeling confused. If the relationship *has* been consummated (which the film seems both to imply and deny), then Merton's demand during carnival night in Venice – copulation in a dark alley – comes across as no more than a momentary whim.

5. On the other hand, the film's supreme triumph – a superb instance of collaboration among screenwriter, director and star – is the vivification and sexualisation of Milly Theale. Leavis put his finger on the novel's central flaw (though I think he gives it too much emphasis at the expense of the book's great strengths – it is, after all, primarily Kate's story, beginning and ending with her): James's Milly, despite all-too-obvious effort, remains an idealised, etherealised blur, sentimentally overvalued by her author. Alison Elliott's amazing performance brings her to vivid and concrete life. Her attraction to Merton, in the novel little more than a 'given', becomes in the film as convincingly sexualised as Kate's. The pallid phantom of the book becomes a young woman of flesh and blood, passionately, physically in love with life even while knowing she is doomed to an early death. Alison Elliott manages the feat of seeming convincingly yet unobtrusively ill even while exuding youthful vitality.

6. The indirect way in which the film reinforces the spectator's emotional commitment to Kate, at the very point where it is most endangered, is the brilliant strategy of having her eventually sabotage her own plot – not, it is true, out of compassion for Milly (it is too late for that), but out of the intensity of her own single-minded commitment to Merton. Lord Mark's visit to Milly in Venice to reveal the truth (out of spite – he, also after Milly's money, has proposed and been rejected) is in the novel, but

there Kate is not responsible for setting it up: the irony of her
intervention in her own scheme is the inspiration of the film-makers. We
see her sudden anxiety at the very moment her plot seems about to
work: during the carnival she sees Merton and Milly embracing, and
instantly grasps the possibility that he might genuinely fall in love with
her. When she returns to England, leaving Merton to fulfil her scheme
and having assured Milly that she feels nothing for him beyond
friendship, the possibility haunts her to the point where, in desperation
and panic, she sends for Lord Mark and tells him the truth, knowing
that he will promptly reveal it to Milly. She has already symbolically
rejected Aunt Maud (by giving her father the necklace Maud presented
her with for her trip to Venice); she now, rather than risk losing Merton,
undermines her own chosen method of gaining money.

7. Charlotte Rampling's Aunt Maud (or Mrs Lowder in the novel, the
name suggesting the character's essential vulgarity) scarcely evokes
James's (and Kate's) image of her as 'Britannia of the marketplace',
and there is no suggestion that she is a widow. However, despite
Rampling's beauty, elegance and external sophistication, the character
becomes *more* vulgar (because more direct) than her original. She is in
fact another aspect of the film's 'melodramatisation' of the novel. In
both book and film she is fully aware of Kate's involvement with
Merton, but her way of handling this problem is very different. James's
Maud, subtler and more devious, at once militant and diplomatic,
provisionally accepts the relationship, allowing Merton access to the
house ('"You may receive, my dear, whom you like" – that was what
Aunt Maud, who in general objected to people's doing what they liked,
had replied; and it bore, this unexpectedness, a good deal of looking
into'). Her assumption is twofold: that any direct veto would merely
exacerbate Kate's obstinacy; and that, since she herself sees the young
man as an unattractive proposition, Kate, with all the temptations of a
life of luxury and an entrée into the 'best' society, will soon tire of him
if allowed for the moment to have her way. The film, on the other
hand, has Maud spying on their secret meetings (obviously not in
person, but we find that she knows all about them) and delivering Kate

an ultimatum: Maud will drop her if she ever sees Merton again. I have no complaints about the change in characterisation, which works well within the context of the film. If there is a problem it occurs to one only in retrospect: if Maud (equipped with Rampling's beauty and relative youthfulness of appearance and manner) is so desirous of bringing a Lord into the family, why doesn't she 'land' one for herself?

Kate

Kate is clearly the crux, and the central problem, for both novelist and film-makers. The great danger is that she will come to be read as a mere villainess. James shows himself acutely aware of this, going so far as to permit himself – quite against his aesthetic principles – a direct authorial address to the reader: 'It may be declared for Kate, at all events, that her sincerity about her friend [i.e. Milly] through this time was deep, her compassionate imagination strong; and that these things gave her a virtue, a good conscience, a credibility for herself, so to speak, that were later to be precious to her' (p. 287).

Kate must be shown genuinely to care for Milly's happiness (brief as it will necessarily – and conveniently – be), to the extent that she can believe that her scheme to gain control of Milly's money when she dies is conceived as much in Milly's interest as in her own; she must believe that in giving her Merton for an indeterminate but brief period she is offering her friend the happiness for which she thirsts, and she must believe this strongly enough to override her own knowledge that the 'happiness' will be built precariously on duplicity and pretence.

This entails a further, more specific, problem, a challenge to the technique of both author and film-makers: how, exactly, does Kate's scheme form itself? – at what precise point does it become fully conscious? – how does one show it evolving from a vague, intuitively grasped, possibility into a deliberate and fully conscious strategy?

This is clearly the aspect of the novel that links it most strongly to *The Golden Bowl*. Kate, while her position in the novel parallels most closely that of Charlotte Stant, anticipates Maggie Verver as a study in the ways in which conscious decisions are determined by unconscious or semi-conscious perceptions, and in the ability of people to deceive themselves as to the morality, motivation and full implications of their actions. Part of the reason why *The Golden Bowl* is so much more difficult to read than the already formidable *The Wings of the Dove* is that it is only in the later novel that James fully confronts this challenge: choosing to narrate so much of it through Maggie's consciousness, he is forced into the near impossible position of having to *imply* the workings of the unconscious through a meticulous analysis of the conscious. In the earlier novel he sidesteps this perhaps insoluble technical problem (whether it is solved in *The Golden Bowl* is certainly open to debate). Kate seems to be introduced in Book 1 as the novel's central consciousness, but James subsequently divides most of the narration between the consciousnesses of Merton and Milly. We watch Kate primarily through their eyes, so that the stages in the evolution of her scheme can be glided over (if intermittently implied). Hence, perhaps, the need for explicit commentary like that quoted above.

The film is bolder: it makes Kate plainly its central character, its consistent centre of interest. At the same time, however, the attitude it defines seems less complex than ambivalent: there are moments when she hovers perilously on the verge of appearing the traditional 'bad woman' of melodrama. In this context, Helena Bonham Carter's own statement (widely quoted in the popular press) seems particularly unfortunate: she told her interviewers how much she had enjoyed playing 'the Bette Davis role'. She may have meant by this (and I hope this is the case) only that she was playing a strong woman, though in fact she always does. But, while Davis's career covers a very wide range of strong women (from *Marked Woman* through *Dark Victory* and *The Great Lie* to *Storm Centre* and *The Corn Is Green*), the popular notion of 'the Bette Davis role' is solidly based on *Jezebel*, *The Letter* and *The Little Foxes*, and was summed up in the famous advertising slogan for *In This Our Life*: 'Bette is never so good as when she's bad.'

I shall centre my examination of the first part of the film (the sequences preceding the move to Venice) on its presentation of Kate and its efforts to do the character justice. But I may as well, here, to get it out of the way, deal briefly with the only moment of the film that worries me deeply, its last: I hated the ending on first viewing. Subsequent viewings have qualified this, but I still see it essentially as a betrayal of everything that has gone before. I have even been tempted (though I know it would be cheating) to make a video of the film from the laserdisc for my own personal viewing, editing out the last two shots, ending on the close-up of Linus Roache's face.

James himself supplied the perfect ending, with one of the greatest last lines in the history of fiction, and it is one place where fidelity would surely have been an asset: after the final confrontation between Kate and Merton in his apartment, after Merton's failure to answer her demand that he is not in love with Milly's memory (which the film faithfully reproduces), he asks if they cannot now return to the relationship 'as we were'. Kate, in the doorway, about to leave, closing the door behind her, responds 'We shall never be again as we were'. It is the moment toward which, we can see in retrospect, the entire novel has moved, the summation of its tragic sense, and it finally clinches our sense of Kate as its tragic heroine. To substitute for this Merton's morbid return to Venice is to replace James's despairingly bleak ending with a sentimental cliché (almost, if not quite, as ridiculous as Rob Morrow's visit to the Taj Mahal at the end of *Last Dance*). Worse, it also tends to redeem Merton at Kate's expense, adding to the conventionally sexist implication that 'it was all the woman's fault'. I would be interested to learn whose decision it represents, and whether anyone protested: it comes across as a stereotypical case of 'studio imposition'.

Before Milly

The film's first image (after the first black-on-white credits) is of shimmering nocturnal reflections on dark water. Most obviously it anticipates Venice (and is briefly recapitulated at the start of the Venice section); more importantly, it suggests at once surface and depth, shifting patterns, uncertainty, instability. We are then (as the credits continue over the images) immediately introduced to Kate, on a platform of the London Underground, as a train arrives. There follows the chance encounter and passionate reunion with Merton, after what we subsequently deduce is a separation of several months, since the death of Kate's mother and her adoption by Aunt Maud. (There is a scene on the Underground in the novel but its function and context are quite different. It registers their second meeting and confirms the mutual attraction they experienced at their first, but they are far short of any embrace or even endearments, Merton simply walking Kate home, the perfect gentleman, to her aunt's house.) Kate's ambivalence – not about her feelings for Merton, but about the viability of their relationship – is immediately established: she abruptly breaks off their erotic embrace in the elevator, responding to his pleading 'Kate…' with a firm 'Merton, no.'

The remainder of the film's first movement (up to the first appearance of Milly Theale) is devoted to establishing and developing three major (and closely interrelated) concerns centred on Kate.

'I won't let you make the same mistake as your mother.' 'I won't be responsible for you. Or your father.'

1. The authenticity and intensity of her commitment to Merton. Their scenes together – in the park (rowing, caught in a sudden downpour, soaked and sheltering within a marble cupola), and in Merton's rooms – develop the ambivalence of the Underground scene but leave no doubt as to the reality of Kate's feelings. They also underline the source of potential discord and (on Merton's side) doubt: he, presumably with some faith in his future as a journalist, is prepared to take the risk of marriage; she cannot face the idea of a future of poverty. This movement culminates (preparing for Milly's entrance into the narrative) in Kate's misery and despair, sobbing alone on her bed when Aunt Maud delivers her ultimatum ('If you ever see your friend again I can't be responsible for you…') and she attempts to break with Merton, watching from her window as he demands admission and is turned away, told by the footman that Kate 'doesn't want to see' him.

2. Kate's father and the dread of poverty. James frankly makes the point that Kate is seduced by the luxury of her aunt's house and her own benefits there, the 'ribbons and silks and velvets', and especially 'the charming quarters her aunt had assigned her', the sense of privacy. The film doesn't dwell on this explicitly, but *shows* it clearly enough in the contrast between her present and the implied past: her father's failure and disgrace, the misery of the marriage for the mother with whom Kate was strongly identified and whose gravestone we see her assiduously cleaning (a splendidly concise and concrete way of showing what the novel states). James opens the novel with her visit to her

'How long do you think you would last without money?'

father and her desperate effort to break off with Maud and live with him, setting it in his 'vulgar little room' in the 'vulgar little street'. The film stages this much later, initially in the more melodramatically vivid and sordid setting of a rowdy and squalid pub where she tracks him down (obviously it was one of his refuges from the marriage and his guilt) in the company of two women, probably prostitutes, then subsequently in his shabby room. Her motive for wanting to leave her aunt (this is before Maud has delivered her ultimatum) is partly her fear of surrendering to temptation: she is fully aware that the relationship with Merton is the most important thing in her life, but the pull of wealth and comfort is strong, and she is afraid Maud will succeed in marrying her 'to someone I don't love'. The father's response is automatic and decisive: 'How long would you last without money?…How long did [your mother and I] last?…It was living like that that killed her.' But the clincher comes in his abrupt revelation that, although Maud has forbidden Kate to see him, he is another of her dependants: she is paying him to leave Kate alone. Maud's subsequent threat that, if Kate sees Merton again, she will 'not be responsible' for her ends with 'or your father'. There follows immediately Kate's refusal to see Merton when he comes to the house, and her collapse on the bed in grief.

3. The humiliation of life with Aunt Maud. Maud's interest in Kate clearly lies less in what she can do for her niece than in what her niece can do for her – though in practical terms the two amount to the same. Kate is young (twenty-three in the novel, convincingly confirmed by Bonham Carter's marvellous performance, combining a knowing worldliness that comes from her background with the youthful energy and idealism it threatens to corrupt), beautiful and amenable to grooming for a role in 'society'. She is an eminently eligible bride when supported by the availability of Maud's highly visible wealth, and a conveniently near relative and ward. Her mother (Maud's sister) dead, her highly inconvenient father bought off in exchange for his invisibility, Kate will not only be a credit to Maud, an adornment for the admiration of her circle, but her means of access to higher

echelons. The husband she has selected is Lord Mark (Alex Jennings), possessor of a London house and a country castle but financially strapped. Maud is introduced supervising Kate's make-up and fastening a diamond necklace about her neck – a motif familiar from other films, most notably *Letter from an Unknown Woman* (where the donor is the heroine's husband) and *Notorious* (where the necklace, like the heroine, is 'rented for the occasion'). An image of possession and control: Kate, like Alicia in *Notorious*, is effectively being prostituted, under cover of respectability. Maud's elegance is exceeded only by her genteel brutality and ruthlessness.

On one level, how can Maud's adoption of her niece seem other than a godsend? Despite the advances of the suffragette movement, upper-class women in early twentieth century Britain were not expected to earn their own living, were trained for little beyond wife- and motherhood. One possible reaction to Kate today – 'Why the hell doesn't she go out and get a job?' – is thoroughly ahistorical and inappropriate. *What* job, anyway? About the only acceptably genteel position for a young woman fallen on hard times through no fault of her own was that of governess, a position for which Kate – strong, impetuous, impatient, and deeply in love – seems singularly ill- equipped. Bonham Carter brilliantly conveys both Kate's awareness of the seductive power of wealth and her constant discomfort and sense of entrapment.

Milly: Attraction and Temptation

From Kate prone and wretched on her bed, and with the background to her situation fully established, we cut abruptly to 'Three months later' and the apparent means of resolving her quandary. At one of Aunt Maud's dinner parties, an unknown woman's voice is heard from offscreen: 'We arrived in London yesterday. I'm so glad we're here. Milly looks completely transformed.' The woman is Susan Shepherd (Elizabeth McGovern), Milly's devoted companion. Kate is next to Lord Mark, dressed in black, 'placed', clearly, by her aunt but in mourning for her relationship with Merton, now seemingly aborted. Kate's and Milly's eyes meet across the table, their faces registering instant mutual interest and attraction. At this stage Kate knows nothing of Milly: their spontaneous recognition of each other *precedes* Lord Mark's description of her ('She'd be Queen of America if they had one. She's the world's richest orphan'). After dinner it is Milly who approaches Kate, in the manner of a seduction ('I finally got you on your own'). Initially, at least, it is not Kate who pursues Milly. The basis of the mutual attraction, with its muted lesbian undertones which subsequent scenes will subtly develop, might be explained in terms of 'opposites attract': Kate, short, petite, dark-haired, pallid, poised, circumspect, always speaking and acting with a certain deliberation (if often impulsively); Milly, tall, red-haired, deceptively robust, vivacious, direct and spontaneous – there is no suggestion yet that her situation is even more desperate than Kate's. Each has her own distinctive beauty: the casting, even apart from the actresses' skills, is

Milly and Kate: at first glance.

wonderfully apt. Milly complains that Lord Mark has been 'monopolising' Kate 'all evening', to which Kate responds 'Yes, but he's been looking at you the whole time.' The note of yearning in Milly's voice is unmistakable: 'So have I.' Milly's beauty lies in the very openness that makes her so vulnerable, in the candour with which she expresses her desire for Kate's friendship, in the naturalness and directness that contrasts so strongly with the corruptness of Aunt Maud and Lord Mark, and with Kate's guardedness and acquired, precarious sophistication. The scene ends with the two women discussing Maud and her plots. Milly: 'You make her sound like a witch.' Kate: 'Oh no. She can't fly. Yet.' Their shared laughter is underscored by Milly's admiring, almost adoring, look at Kate.

Separating the sequences of Kate's first two encounters with Milly is the very brief scene at her mother's grave, where she scrubs the headstone: the strategy is to heighten sympathy for Kate by emphasising her capacity for commitment and her sense of loss, at the exact point where her behaviour begins to take on suspect overtones. When she sees Milly again (from the top of an open double-decker bus) it is Kate who takes the initiative. At the beginning of the scene she knows no more about Milly's situation than that she is extremely rich, and when she calls to her from the bus she cannot possibly have formed any 'plot' (turning herself into a potential witch, like her aunt). The most we can suspect is that her attraction (conscious? intuitive?) is not only to a clearly lovable young woman but to the desirability of acquiring a wealthy friend. The immediate sequel, however, gives her her first intimation of Milly's predicament. We see Milly, oblivious to Kate's call, put a slip of paper (which we, and Kate, may presume to be a prescription or a notice of a further appointment) into her handbag. Kate crosses the street to read the nameplate on the building Milly has just left: 'Sir Luke Strett, consultant'.

She follows Milly into a bookstore, confronting her somewhat aggressively with 'I thought you were running away from me', although it seems clear to us (and must also be to Kate) that Milly, obviously preoccupied, neither saw nor heard her. Kate then asks whom she was visiting. Milly lies ('Some friends'), looking down with an evasive smile, which clearly suggests a problem serious enough to be kept a secret. Kate

promptly leads her to the pornography section at the rear of the
bookstore, swiftly clearing out its all-male clientele ('Excuse me, is this the
foreign language section?'). She opens a book, apparently at random, and
invites Milly to enjoy with her one of the illustrations, an image of
complicated three-way sex involving two women and a man: one woman
is prone on her back on a bed, her legs hanging down over the side; the
second is kneeling over her, bending her head; the man is licking between
the second woman's buttocks. It is one of the film's oddest and most
tantalising moments, for what does it tell us about Kate? She is
presumably familiar with this section of the store, at least to the point of
knowing where it is situated (we must not assume that she frequents it!).
She appears to open the book at random, though its image is clearly
apposite (to the narrative, not to the immediate scene): two women
sharing one man, combining lesbian and heterosexual relations. A fantasy

The erotic picture. The women's response.

of how things might, ideally, be worked out among the three central characters (though figurative rather than literal), a premature utopian solution to what later coalesces into a situation soluble only in tragedy? But Milly, at this stage, has not even set eyes on Merton, let alone fallen in love with him, while Kate has (officially at least) broken off their relationship. We seem at this point to be looking at the film's unconscious rather than at Kate's. And what does Milly's quite unselfconscious pleasure in the image, she and Kate joining in a laughter that seems at once satirical and complicit, tell us about her? Certainly that we are not to take Alison Elliott's Milly as an attempted faithful representation of James's sheltered and artificially innocent heroine: the radiant and authentic innocence of the film's Milly is not dependent upon the suppression of knowledge or a carefully guarded, inhibition-generating upbringing. One might suppose that here Kate is testing Milly, assessing how far and how swiftly she can go, but that is to assume that she is already following some fully evolved plan. Rather, it is one of those moments in the film that seem to offer a fully dramatised equivalent of James's 'late' preoccupation: the way in which impulses are prompted by shadowy motivations not yet accessible to consciousness.

From the bookstore and the women's laughter we are thrown abruptly into yet another party, the third in the film (apparently Lord Mark's, as he appears to be acting as host), perhaps the same evening. The two young women are side by side on a sofa, Lord Mark on a chair to their left, so that Kate is in the middle. She remains silent throughout this

Lord Mark's party.

mini-scene, while her two companions talk over her and about her. Lord
Mark is expressing a half-serious outrage at their transgression of the
proprieties ('If I'd been the owner I'd have thrown you out… You saw the
pictures'); Milly indignantly defends their rights ('I saw them. Have I
suddenly become corrupt?'). The film's Milly, with her 'shocking'
knowledge and unspoiled innocence, more resembles the Nanda
Brookenham of *The Awkward Age* than her more obvious counterpart
Maggie Verver. Lord Mark's response ('It's a gradual process. Look at
Kate') is, even more indignantly, rejected by Milly ('There's nothing
corrupt about Kate'), while Kate sits silent between them with an
enigmatic smile. It's another tantalising moment, rich in uncertainties:
Lord Mark, himself thoroughly corrupt and dissolute, we already guess to
be in love with Kate (a soulmate in corruption?) – a guess fully confirmed
by the subsequent episode in his castle. How just, at this point, do we feel
his perception of her to be? – and how seriously intended is the
perception, spoken casually, as if in (somewhat drunken) jest? Does
Kate's silence represent an implicit acknowledgment of the accuracy of his
assessment of her? Does her confidence that she can leave Milly to
repudiate it presage her subsequent abuse of her friend's trust?

The women leave Lord Mark (with Milly's parting 'I think we're
going to leave you until you've sobered up'), apparently separating briefly.
Merton arrives with an older woman, to whom he has attached himself in
order to gate-crash the party. We see Milly watching from an upstairs
balcony, instantly interested, her immediate instinctive attraction echoing
her first view of Kate. Then Kate appears behind her. It is clear that
Milly's first glimpse of Merton has not been engineered by Kate, who
couldn't have known he was coming (they haven't seen each other since
her enforced rejection of him) – any more than she could have engineered
the subsequent chance encounter with Merton in the art gallery. Neither
has Kate the least reason to assume that Milly would be instantly attracted
to him (indeed, it places a certain strain on the viewer's credulity!). The
film is at pains to confirm that there is so far no diabolical plot. Kate does,
however, hasten to describe Merton (in answer to Milly's query) as 'a
friend of the family', implicitly denying any personal interest. The

response appears spontaneous and improvised, but its dishonesty suggests some underlying, half-conscious motive. The main import of this entire segment, however, is to reaffirm the genuineness of Kate's commitment to Merton: when she lures him to the privacy of an upstairs billiards room and is confronted with his defensive bitterness, we cannot doubt the sincerity of her '*I* hurt. So much. You can't imagine.' She kisses him passionately, then sends him back to the woman he came with and whom he publicly kissed for Kate's benefit: 'I want you to go back and kiss her. With that mouth... I'll come and see you soon.'

It is the next two scenes that chart the development in Kate from subconscious promptings to fully conscious decisions – the formation of a definite plan out of a vague and undefined sense of possibilities. First, Kate and Milly, in a taxi, discuss their joint invitation to Lord Mark's castle. Milly tells Kate he 'isn't my type'; when Kate asks who is, she mentions Merton. We see Kate pondering this, the possibilities crystallising. Then Kate, keeping her promise to visit Merton, surprises him in his newspaper office. They discuss his exposé of corruption in the medical profession, which gives Kate the opening she needs to ask him what he knows about Sir Luke Strett, and Merton tells her that he's 'a famous blood specialist'. This leads immediately to Kate's informing Merton casually that Milly 'likes' him. Merton's lack of interest is plain in his self-deprecating dismissal: 'That's because she doesn't know me.'

We pass to Milly, undergoing further tests with Sir Luke, who tells her 'Everything's going to be fine.' Alison Elliott's marvellously expressive face tells us just how seriously she takes such platitudinous reassurance. The camera tracks from her over what looks, today, like very primitive equipment, coming to rest on a glass sphere; there is an abrupt cut to another sphere, a football falling from the sky right into camera. It is the one moment in an otherwise delicate and subtle film that seems a surrender to the temptation of an opportunistic 'shock' effect, though I suppose it might be rationalised as a rude awakening from Sir Luke's lulling pacifications. Milly is in a park watching a group of young boys playing football. She is quite alone, and presumably has come straight from Sir Luke's office. She comes forward, applauding, pathetically calling out

'Wonderful': the moment obliquely suggests her sense of aloneness and desolation, her immediate need for any form of human contact. The boys shy away, awkward and embarrassed, not knowing what to make of the inappropriate and painfully self-conscious intrusion by a strange young woman into their world. A thunderstorm interrupts further play.

Milly hurries for the only visible shelter, a small art gallery in the park housing an extensive exhibition of paintings by Klimt. (The gallery is the Serpentine in Kensington Gardens.) Milly studies an erotic portrayal of a pair of lovers, of whom the dominant figure is strikingly androgynous – we can't tell for sure (except perhaps from a prior knowledge of the artist) whether male or female. We see Kate pass by in distant long shot through the doorway to the next room, followed by Merton a few paces behind, though Milly sees only the latter, and follows him. Kate calls out, then promptly organises them into looking together at a portrait of a voluptuous nude. Merton, making polite conversation, remarks 'Kate's been talking about you all afternoon' – after which he discreetly withdraws, leaving the two women together. Kate tells Milly 'It's not what you're thinking.' Milly is sceptical: 'No?' Kate insists that 'he's an old family friend'. Milly looks very uncertain.

Cut to Lord Mark shooting at (and missing) rabbits from the turrets of his castle. It is early morning but he is already (or still?) somewhat drunk. Milly and Kate appear in their dressing-gowns, awakened by the racket, and clearly disturbed and repelled by his impotent violence. The brief scene intensifies our sense of his unpleasantness, and the frustration and desperation that underlie it: what sense of identity he possesses depends entirely upon his status, his castle, his London mansion. It therefore prepares us for one of the film's crucial scenes – crucial, especially, for Kate: his nocturnal visit to her bedroom and its effect upon her.

We see him first in his drawing-room, drinking again – because he is an alcoholic, but also because he is trying to pluck up his courage. Everyone else is asleep. He sneaks into Kate's room and, in the dark, feels her body under the covers. When Kate wakes, and tells him to leave immediately, he reveals his full intentions. He loves Kate but he must have money, he is in danger of losing his castle; Milly is dying ('Everyone in

New York knows about it') so he will marry her (her millions, presumably, a more adequate alternative to Aunt Maud's hundreds of thousands), but 'when she's gone…'. Kate's shock transcends any indignation at being sexually harassed by an unwanted and drunken suitor in her bed in the middle of the night: it is her great moment of self-recognition. Her startled look isn't feigned: she has not allowed herself, up to this point, to formulate the idea that Milly might actually *marry* Merton, and she has not known for certain just how serious Milly's condition is. But it is precisely this possibility that Mark's ugly and heartless outburst brings to the surface. She is forced to see herself reflected in a man she thoroughly despises.

The immediate sequel is one of the film's finest inspirations: Kate goes to Milly's room to sleep with her, on the pretext that her room is too cold ('These wretched aristocrats can't even heat their houses'). Her

Nocturnal intrusion: 'I need Milly's money.' The shared bed: Kate's disturbance.

motivation is extremely complex, and the film, here as elsewhere, withholds any limiting explanation, refusing to simplify. Kate is deeply disturbed – who better to turn to for the comfort she needs than the dear friend who she knows will be more than ready to give it? But she must also reassure herself of her genuine affection for Milly, the one thing that distinguishes her from Lord Mark. Is it also, at a level Kate cannot allow to become quite conscious, a further move to increase her intimacy with Milly, to gain her complete trust and love? Significantly, Kate has not uttered a word about the event that prompted her visit: to tell Milly about Lord Mark's confession would bring her uncomfortably close to her own secret, which we are watching in the very process of formation. Kate (unwilling, perhaps, to get too close emotionally to the woman whose trust she is planning to betray) turns away, but Milly snuggles up, puts her arm around her, and Kate covers Milly's hand with her own. Milly's charm, as we have already seen, lies largely in her lack of inhibition, what may strike us as a rare survival into womanhood of the infant's 'polymorphous perversity' (among Freud's finest concepts, though his terminology is most unfortunate: how can the natural state of the uncorrupted infant be described as 'perverse'?). The sequence closes with the camera moving in on Kate's face, as she looks down at the hand, emblem of unquestioning trust, clasped in her own, Bonham Carter eloquently expressing the character's profound disturbance and confusion as she confronts the full implications of the temptation into which she has allowed herself to slip.

The remainder of this first movement develops the tensions that have been accumulating to the point where Kate – immediately prior to the move to Venice – makes her decisive and irrevocable choice, suppressing all her (well-founded) qualms about the moral implications and possible consequences of what she is doing. The steps to this involve the three people who have determined Kate's actions, giving us the last appearances in the film (but not in the novel) of two of them.

   Merton. Kate's manipulation of the man she loves continues with a luncheon that she sets up but fails to attend, leaving Merton (hopefully) with Milly and Susan Shepherd. It is the first time she actually engineers an encounter. Indignant, he leaves, but not before Milly has revealed the fact of the women's imminent departure for Venice, of which Merton apparently knew nothing. She invites him to come too, to which he responds, ironically but not unkindly, 'That's something only a princess would say.'

There follows a confrontation on the stairs to Merton's apartment: 'Where were you?' 'Here.' 'Then why was I there?… You didn't just stand me up, you *set* me up.' They discuss the trip to Venice: told of Milly's invitation, Kate encourages him to join them, then asks whether he doesn't think Milly is beautiful. To his negative reply she tells him 'I think she's the most beautiful woman I've ever met.' Merton: 'Then I'm sure you'll have a good time in Venice.' The scene raises (but doesn't clearly answer) the question of what Merton actually suspects. He has grasped that Kate is trying to 'set up' something involving himself and Milly; he doesn't know about Milly's illness. His final utterance, while it can be read as mere sarcasm, can also be read as a suspicion, supported by the women's very evident mutual enjoyment of each other's company, that Kate may be interested in Milly as more than a friend, and that she is trying to set up some form of three-way relationship. Merton's subsequent shock, in Venice, when he is finally confronted with what Kate is really up to, may initially seem unconvincing, but it is reasonable enough in the context of the women's attachment to each other and his own simplicity, openness and idealism.

Aunt Maud. The final appearance in the film of Aunt Maud (who, in the novel, accompanies the women to Venice) establishes Kate's sense of the possibility of gaining her independence and, as a corollary, Maud's anxious awareness of a weakening in her control of her niece. Maud's anxiety expresses itself in an unwary cruelty and desire to humiliate which we may take to be decisive in Kate's subsequent actions. At the beginning of the scene Maud is still objecting to the Venice expedition, where Kate will be beyond her control, though her actions show that she has already resigned herself to it. She attempts a veiled threat, to which Kate responds, defiantly, 'Then I'll have to ask Milly for help.' Maud's bitter 'It didn't take you long to find a new patron' elicits the instant, defensive 'She's a friend.' To which Maud retorts 'Call it what you will, you're still for hire.' There follows the desperate bribe of a diamond necklace and matching bracelet, but Maud can't resist alienating her niece even further: 'You'll need something nice to wear around Milly. People might think you're her servant.'

Kate's father. The film cuts to Kate on the Underground once again, surreptitiously fingering the jewels. Her destination is the opium den she clearly knows her father frequents (her familiarity with his haunts underlining the unsavouriness of the background from which Maud extricated her). She leaves the jewels at the door, with instructions that they be delivered, and we watch him unwrapping Aunt Maud's misguided attempt to buy back her niece.

For Kate, the act is clearly decisive and final: she is casting off, with a single gesture, both of her sordid entanglements, symbolically breaking with Maud by giving away her precious gift, but also (we assume) breaking with her father by handing over to him an extremely valuable property. Kate can now feel 'clean' – and free to pursue an aim which will prove more morally contaminating than anything from which she has extricated herself.

From Mr Croy bemusedly fingering the jewels the camera moves up to the wall above his head; dissolve to the film's opening image, the shimmering reflections on dark water that signify Venice.

The gift of the jewels.

Intermission

Before plunging into those shimmering surfaces and dark depths I want to take a moment to recapitulate, develop, and then largely abandon an issue central to this monograph, then make good what by this time must seem to readers a very curious omission.

First, the film's relationship to the novel can now be defined more precisely. Narrative film is always, and of necessity, concrete: it has to show people doing and saying things in definite locations. James, in the late novels, is less and less concrete: he goes into meticulous detail about what a character is thinking, but is frequently vague or unhelpful about where s/he is thinking it. If James is to be filmed at all, it is obvious that action, dialogue and decor must replace the pages of analysis of inner perception and reflection. I mentioned earlier that only a very few scenes in the film have even loose equivalents in the novel. First, there is the scene in the Underground, transposed to the start of the film from where it occurs in the book (somewhat later and then only in Kate's memory), its content there being quite different. Second, the scene in Mr Croy's sitting-room, transposed in reverse (it opens the novel), again has different, if not wholly dissimilar, content; and third, the scenes with Aunt Maud bear, if imprecisely, some resemblance to Kate's dealings with her in the novel. All the film's most striking scenes – the bookstore, the art gallery, Lord Mark's nocturnal intrusion and its sequel with the two women in bed together, the scene in Merton's newspaper office, the luncheon for which Kate sets him up, the opium den – have no equivalents in the novel whatever. None of them, on the other hand, is an irrelevancy, and, although James couldn't and wouldn't have written their literary equivalents, none seems to me a betrayal of the book's general themes or overall meaning. The film's brilliance lies in its ability to stand as an autonomous work, and an intensely *creative* one, while remaining faithful to what might be called the novel's core. The film could not have existed without Henry James, yet it exists magnificently in its own right, without evoking more than the most evanescent resemblances and comparisons.

And the omission: in my traversal of the film so far I have managed to reach almost its midpoint without once mentioning the name of its director. The omission is certainly not meant to imply that, like so many nondescript movies, it doesn't effectively have one, that 'it was all in the script' or was 'just flung together': Hossein Amini's extremely intelligent screenplay plus three outstanding leading actors could not add up to *The Wings of the Dove*, which everywhere displays irrefutable evidence of a strong and sensitive controlling, guiding, creating presence. The problem is that as yet I simply don't *know* Iain Softley: I don't know who he is. I have seen his two previous films, *Backbeat* and *Hackers*, twice each, and though *Backbeat*, at least, is of some interest I find it impossible to trace continuities of theme and style. I would never have guessed, without prior knowledge, that they were the work of the same director, and *The Wings of the Dove* seems to me in an altogether different class of achievement. I went to it on its initial release – unusually for me – not because I longed to see another film by the director of *Hackers*, but because I have loved the novel for many years and was curious to see how anyone could possibly film it. I shall go to see Iain Softley's next film the day it opens because it is by the director of *The Wings of the Dove*.

One of the film's many distinctions is Softley's inventive and often expressive use of the full widescreen, in its 2.35:1 ratio, and it seems appropriate here to offer a warning: if you see *The Wings of the Dove* only on video, you will not see the film Softley directed. The writing of this monograph was delayed for some months because the film had vanished from the theatres (and in any case notes scribbled in the dark are scarcely adequate to my purpose) and the laserdisc was held back from distribution long after it had been announced. The video was worse than useless: I switched off after ten minutes, unable to bear what seemed a desecration. It is my opinion that the reduction of widescreen films (by pan-and-scan) should be declared illegal, and punishable by heavy fines. At least today most videos offer a terrible warning, so as soon as you read 'This film has been reformatted to fit your TV screen' you can replace it immediately on the shelf. Unfortunately in many cases it is the only way now that a film (or part of it – roughly two-thirds of each image) can be seen at all.

The second part of this study, then, will contain far fewer references to Henry James and far more analysis of the *mise-en-scène*.

Love and Death in Venice

From the soft-focus shimmering the image shifts into sharp focus on the water of a Venice canal, the camera, tracking right, moving up to reveal the gondolas bearing the two women and their luggage to Milly's palazzo. As they move through the building the women are in long shot, the one small light is extinguished (by the servant Eugenio) at Milly's 'Let's eat in the dark', moonlight dimly illuminating a spacious salon, sparsely but expensively furnished. At Kate's amazed 'Is this all yours?' Milly laughs self-deprecatingly and tells her 'It's *ours.*' In the novel the palazzo is rented; in the film Milly appears to have bought it – she is, after all, 'the world's richest orphan', with only a short time to live, so why not? Her response can also be taken to imply that after her death it will be Kate's – an implication that Kate, of course, is not meant to understand. Much (though by no means all) of the Venice section takes place at night, the *mise-en-scène* built often on images of a small area of light within surrounding darkness or (in the carnival scenes) on moving lights and shimmering shadows, developing the imagery of reflections on dark water.

Milly leads the way out on to the high balcony and tells Kate (not looking into her face) that if she gets bored she can invite anyone she wants. Kate first denies that she could get bored, then abruptly asks 'Who would you like me to invite?' The scene begins in long shot, cuts (on Milly's question) to a somewhat closer two-shot, then, with Kate's response, to a close-up side view of Milly, still looking away over the balcony: 'Whoever you like.' But it is clear to us (and to Kate) that she has someone specific in mind. Cut to close-up of Kate who, after a pause, asks 'Shall I invite Merton?' Milly, smiling, looks down at her hands: 'I already have. He said no.' Kate: 'Do you want *me* to ask him?' Milly hesitates, then looks at Kate for the first time: 'Only if you want to.' Kate: 'Only if *you* want to.' Milly: 'He's *your* friend, I hardly know him.' Kate: 'All right then. We won't ask him.' But she is smiling, and Milly smiles complicitly back, and they laugh. It is a beautifully played little scene, with so much going on beneath the simple dialogue: Milly wanting Merton to come but still afraid there may be more between him and Kate than Kate admits; Kate wanting Milly to persuade her to ask Merton, because she wants

Merton there for herself, because she wants Merton there to make Milly happy, because she needs him there to further her scheme.

Then night. Kate, lying in bed wide awake, hears Milly coughing painfully, Susan hushing and comforting her. Kate watches, unseen, from her doorway as Susan passes with a lamp (to fetch medicine?). Milly coughs again, then breaks down and begins to cry. Kate closes her door. We see her writing to Merton: to make Milly happy? to encourage their relationship? The ambiguity is perfect, giving Kate her self-justification for her actions (because her concern is genuine).

We see Merton reading her letter. He looks as if he's about to tear it up, but Milly's voice is heard over the image: 'Merton, what made you change your mind?' Cut to a narrow, crowded street; the women are accompanying him to his lodging (no romantic gondolas, no grand palazzo, for Merton). The characters remain in long shot, among the crowd, but we continue to hear their voices. Merton: 'Oh, I was always going to come….' Kate: 'Oh, really!' '…It just took me a little time to scrape the money together.' We never get to read Kate's letter, and his decision is never explained, just glossed over. We are fobbed off with his ironic guided tour of his humble, barely furnished, lodgings, a 'bathhouse' which is (Milly jokes) 'modelled after the famous Byzantine bathhouse in Constantinople', but in fact contains only a metal tub as its bathing facility.

Merton is the film's weak link, and his lack of full credibility is by no means the fault of Linus Roache, who does everything that can be done with a highly problematic role. There is an important distinction to be made between the film's treatment of Kate's inner life (meticulously charted, as I have tried to show) and its treatment of Merton's. I questioned earlier the wisdom of the decision to alter Merton's character so drastically from the Merton of the novel, and it is in the Venice sequences that the ensuing problem emerges clearly. One can see why the change was felt necessary. In James's time decency (even when characterised by passivity) and integrity (even when it takes the negative form of refusing to be 'vulgar') were more readily accepted as positive values than they would be today, in a world in which we are not only surrounded by but immersed in vulgarity and exploitation: one has simply

The necklace: 'Try to look as if you'd worn it all your life.' Merton as radical. Kate's father carousing.

Kate after her enforced rejection of Merton. Milly's and Kate's eyes meet.

'It's a gradual process. Look at Kate.' Watching Merton at Lord Mark's party: 'Do you know who he is?' The opium den.

'Shall I ask Merton?' Milly's reaction. Sunshine and symmetry.

The nocturnal gondola ride: journey into darkness and entrapment.

'She's in love with you.' The parapet. Milly's collapse.

'That's why you wanted me to come to Venice. For her.' 'For her … and for us.'

Preparing for the masquerade. The kiss. Kate's reaction.

'If you don't understand me, then I don't understand you.' Milly: 'Please don't lie to *me*.' Kate: 'Please don't lie to me.'

With Kate departed, Merton reluctantly begins the deception. Merton in Venice, Kate in London: rain, doubt, guilt.

'I have a good feeling.' Kate's letter: fear and self-confrontation. 'I told you I was going to make a fool of myself tonight.'

Milly's yearning, Merton's confusion and distress. Kate visits Lord Mark.

Merton refused admission by the ambiguously devoted Eugenio. 'Tell her it isn't true.' 'Did he want to *kill* her?'

Merton's visit to Milly. Milly's love. The letter.

The death of Eros. 'Give me your word of honour … that you aren't in love with her memory.'

Merton's silent answer. False memory. The lost moment of almost harmony.

to ride on a subway (or Underground) train and be assailed by the
ubiquitous advertisements to be aware of this. In such a world James's
Merton would be instantly pigeonholed, by perhaps the majority of
viewers, as a 'wimp', and Kate's passionate commitment to him might well
appear not only misguided and implausible but ridiculous. Hence, I take
it, the decision to change him from a writer of tasteful (though also clearly
intelligent) descriptive literature into an outspoken and audacious leftist
crusader. The decision is of course a very attractive one: it is what, in
today's world, a Merton not only might but ought to become. The
problem is it simply doesn't work in the context of the film. The decision
to come to Venice is not, as we shall see, his only decision that is glossed
over, elided by an abrupt cut.

It is day: sunlight, but the soft blue of the sky suggests late
afternoon. The camera tracks right over water, a church in centre
background, three people in distant long shot seated on the steps leading
down to the water, the gently moving shot accompanied by gentle,
repetitive, minimalist-style music. Cut to opposite view: the three figures,
seen from behind, are Merton, Milly and Kate. A flute melody emphasises
the atmosphere of harmony, as do the perfect weather, the formal group-
shot, the geometrical pattern of the paving, the blue water and the
gondolas in the background. Milly rises to take a photograph; Merton and
Kate move closer, perhaps holding hands.

There follows one of the film's most magical sequences, the
gondola ride. The women's clothes, usually strongly contrasted (Kate's
dark, strong, Milly's soft, pale), are here similar in colouring, Kate's white,
Milly's a softer off-white with brown trimmings. But the sense of harmony
is not undisturbed: Kate, against Merton's protests, unnecessarily hires
two boats, high-handedly organising the party so that she rides in one,
leaving Merton to accompany Milly in the other. The grounds for
Merton's hostility deserve comment, since he doesn't know about Milly's
condition and has not grasped Kate's plan. Yet he is aware that he is being
manipulated – for what purpose? We must assume, I think, some less-
than-clearly-defined anxiety about the women's intimacy and the role
within it that Kate seems to be constructing for him.

The journey through the canals is also a journey into nightfall. The shade, deepening from shot to shot, is accompanied by a sense of 'things closing in', the gondolas passing between high walls, the camera moving back to intensify the sense of enclosure, the boats emerging from a tunnel not to greater openness but to high buildings in near-darkness filmed in oppressive low-angle tracking-shots (perhaps Milly's point of view). The only dialogue at first is the voice of the gondolier/guide. There is a close-up of Milly, her face lit, lying back, looking up with a faint smile, Elliott's remarkably expressive face registering mingled happiness and regret, a yearning for the life she knows is denied her. The sombre atmosphere is broken by the women's playfulness. Kate calls out 'Diego's flirting with me. What's your Italian like Milly?', to which Milly responds, smiling, 'I can't see him in the dark.' The women's laughter contrasts with Merton's silence. Kate calls 'Merton, say something'; his only response is 'You're drunk aren't you?', to which Kate retorts that it's 'not such a bad idea'. As the gondolas enter a narrow passage between buildings Kate calls to Milly to come closer. The gondolas, in distant long shot, are for a moment adjacent, and there is some kind of physical exchange between the two women, leaning close, perhaps kissing each other's hands, affectionate mutual laughter. Merton maintains his silence, a soundless discord.

It's an emotionally complex, delicate, beautiful sequence. The possibility of the achievement of a harmonious three-way relationship is continuously suggested yet continuously disturbed: in narrative content by Merton's refusal to participate, in atmosphere by the progress from day to night, light to darkness, and by the ominous pressure of the high dark buildings. It's another sequence constructed around the little core of light in a surrounding darkness.

It is the next day, and the three (now accompanied by Susan Shepherd) visit St Mark's. Both women are now in blue, Kate's bright, Milly's pale. Milly wants to climb the stairs of the tower and asks each in turn to accompany her, tactfully starting with the two women. Kate 'doesn't like heights'. Susan, the devoted companion, thinks only of her charge ('It's a long way up, Milly. Are you sure?'). Milly turns eagerly to Merton ('Merton, will you come?'), but gets only 'I'm not good with heights either.' Milly goes up alone, disappointed but as always uncomplaining; Susan hesitates, then follows to watch over her. Many have said that Elizabeth McGovern is wasted: certainly it's a self-effacing role, but Susan is a self-effacing character. McGovern beautifully expresses, with very little dialogue to work with, her concern and her devotion. Her performance quietly suggests a lesbian attachment that makes no demands, is content simply to contribute to the comfort and tranquillity of the woman she clearly adores – a tranquillity that will subsequently be disrupted beyond repair.

Meanwhile Merton and Kate walk in the street outside. Kate tells him he should have gone with Milly 'because she asked you to', and accuses him of rudeness; Merton responds with 'Why do you want me to be with her all the time?' Kate first says that she doesn't want Milly to 'feel left out', to which he retorts 'She doesn't care', the clearly insensitive abruptness reasserting his total lack of interest in Milly. Kate: 'Of course she does.' Slight pause; then: 'She's in love with you.' He is incredulous: 'She hardly knows me.' But Kate knows Milly intimately: 'That doesn't matter. It's the way she is.' The brief exchange – almost matter-of-fact, but filled with underlying tension – is important for its confirmation of what has already been hinted: Kate's hardening. The plot she formed and believes herself to control has begun to take her over, to *replace* her feelings for others, she is becoming insensitive not only to Milly but to Merton. The film is extremely shrewd about the insidious fascination of the power to manipulate, its destructiveness not only for others but for the self.

Cut to the parapet of St Mark's, tracking-shot forward, tilt down on to the square beneath, revealed immediately as Milly's point of view, then an extreme long shot from the square, her pale blue dress just visible, then back to Milly leaning over. It is tempting to embark here on a further hymn to Alison Elliott: she is, I think, quite extraordinary in her ability to communicate the character's mixed emotions – delight, exhilaration, despair, joy in living combined with full awareness of her condition (mopping throat and face with a handkerchief after her impetuous exertions). Milly looks as if she might just possibly throw herself off, despite her delight in being alive. Then Susan appears behind her. Milly turns, smiles reassuringly; Susan smiles back.

The mopping of throat and face presages the progress of the following (continuous) scenes: a fish market, where Milly is overcome by fatigue and where the dead fish and assorted sea-creatures appear (from her point of view) increasingly ugly and disgusting; a boat ride along a crowded, narrow canal where Milly has a 'dizzy spell', dabs her face and throat with canal water, then almost falls over when the boat collides with another, Merton catching her as she falls; a hospital, where Susan tells Kate and Merton 'Nothing to worry about. She's asleep.'

Yet, for all the film's emotional investment in Milly, Kate remains its central figure: one might say that it is structured on her decisions. The decision of the next scene equals, in structural significance, her decision to give Aunt Maud's precious jewels to her father. We are in a simple canal-side eating place. A slow right-to-left pan over passing gondolas reveals Kate and Merton at a table, the pan becoming a slow track-in. Kate tells Merton that Milly is dying. From 'Milly's dying'/'She can't be. She looks fine,' the remainder of the scene cross-cuts between them. At first the camera tracks slowly in on each as they speak, Kate seeming to be sounding him out, judging how far she can go, then, at the precise moment when Merton (answering Kate's 'She doesn't want our pity') asks 'What *does* she want?' the forward tracks are replaced by static shot/reverse shot head-and-shoulders close-ups. We don't see the two together again in the frame throughout the rest of the scene, the physical separation emphasising the developing tension as Merton begins to understand just what is going on. But the scene ends abruptly at the moment when Merton fully grasps Kate's plan – the moment when the Merton established in the film's first half would surely get up, walk out, and leave Venice. John Ford was once asked in an interview (*Stagecoach* being the film in question) why the Indians didn't shoot the lead horses: 'Because that would have been the end of the film.' But the objection here is more serious: damage is being done to the integrity of a leading character.

How do we take Kate's response to 'That's why you wanted me to come to Venice. For her': 'For her…[long pause] And for us'? She feels compelled to look away on the second clause – we see her thinking, deciding whether this is the strategic moment to at last be honest with him. I have the feeling that both clauses are genuine, that she still holds on to a belief that she is furthering Milly's happiness. Yet we know, from previous hints, that the latter clause has now taken precedence, that Kate's plot has taken her over, that her strength is degenerating into ruthlessness.

But this is followed immediately by a beautiful, wordless scene of the women's intimacy. Kate is seated, Milly is standing behind her arranging her hair; both are in white nightdresses, both appear happy and contented. Yet the scene is darkly lit, the only light the table lamp, surrounded by deep shadow. The sequence consists of only two takes, the women in long shot throughout; the camera tracks, then circles slightly, left to right, slowly and steadily, with items of decor (a candelabra and other ornaments) intervening in the foreground – an Ophuls shot, graceful, decorative, tender, at once loving and distant. An intrusive pillar brings a momentarily darkened screen, permitting a concealed cut; when the camera re-emerges into light it is somewhat closer, and further to the left, though it continues the steady left-right movement. Both women are now seated, Kate applying Milly's lipstick for her.

Cut to exterior, the camera still tracking/circling but now right to left, over a canal at nightfall where gondolas are gathered. A cut to closer reveals their occupants in sinister Phantom-of-the-Opera type white masks: it is carnival night, the explanation for the women's preparations. Cut to a shot looking down from the top of the canalside steps, which the characters are now mounting, Milly in a white dress, white mask, Kate very dashing in a trim little black moustache and black matador costume, Merton wearing a sombrero. He tells them 'We'll go over to the bridge': it is the bridge to crowds and chaos, where anyone might get lost. Milly rips off her mask (she never wears masks, unlike Kate). Everyone is in fancy dress, there is a band playing Italian music but wearing gipsy costumes (suggesting, according to stereotype, licence and abandonment). Milly, at last taking the initiative, invites Merton to dance, and as they dance she tells him 'You don't look yourself today… You look wounded. Your eyes are big and sad.' In the

presumably short period since Kate's revelations (but Milly has had time to
recover) he has accepted her project and is bearing the consequences, a
burden of guilt and deceit. Kate watches, Merton favours her with a
complicit smile, which she returns uneasily; she has also shed her
moustache, perhaps unconsciously wanting to retain her femininity, a
further suggestion of uneasiness. Milly asks 'Would you rather be dancing
with *her*?', and Merton (who clearly would) slightly overplays his role: 'With
Kate?' (as if the idea were absurd)… 'I'm perfectly happy dancing with
you.' But his tone lacks all sense of intimacy, the words sound insincere, as
if spoken out of enforced politeness. Milly laughs: 'You're a beautiful liar' –
with a slight stress on 'beautiful', suggesting not merely 'beautiful liar' but
'beautiful man'. When the dance ends they pause a moment, then Milly
leans forward and kisses him on the mouth; he doesn't resist. Cut to Kate
watching, her uneasiness now very clear: it has suddenly occurred to her
that her plot could work all too well (didn't she herself put it into Merton's
head that Milly is the most beautiful woman she's ever met?). Cut to a
circular group dance, Milly and Merton holding hands, the increasing
wildness underlined by zip-pans. Kate's disturbance increases: she is
confronting for the first time the actual physical possibility of Merton and
Milly having a sexual relationship, and of Merton no longer having to
pretend to be in love. (This is a complete departure from the novel, where
the possibility seems never to occur to her until after Milly's death. It is
clearly a consequence of the film's rethinking of Milly as a vivacious and
fully sexual woman far removed from James's idealised 'princess', and
made flesh by the inspired casting.)

  Milly stops to bathe her face and throat in a fountain, calling to them
to wait for her, but Kate impetuously leads Merton off, with near-disastrous
consequences, answering Merton's objection ('We'll lose them') with a
succinct and emphatic 'Good.' We see Milly and Susan searching, Milly
hopefully declaring that 'They're probably waiting for us back at the
fountain.' Susan says nothing, but McGovern's face is eloquent: she has
guessed the truth about Kate and Merton but hasn't the heart to disillusion
Milly. There have been indications (including 'You're a beautiful liar') that
Milly also knows but rejects the knowledge, needing the illusion.

Kate leads Merton to a dark and deserted alley and tells him frankly 'I thought I'd lost you tonight.' They embrace, Merton passionate with desire. But Kate's mind is on other things: 'This is the first time I didn't feel sorry for her…She was so happy dancing with you.' This is the first time we have seen Kate confused, torn between the obsessive pursuit of her plan and fear of its possible consequences. She responds to Merton's increasing physical insistence by telling him 'I'd better leave you alone with her.' Hurt by her coldness, he first rebels against her scheme, demands that Kate make love, then, when she refuses ('I don't understand'), resorts to emotional blackmail: 'If you don't understand me, then I don't understand you.' Cut to Milly and Susan by the fountain, Milly looking beaten and exhausted, but insisting that 'They'll come back here' when Susan tries to make her give up. Cut back to Kate and Merton copulating against a wall.

This is perhaps the film's most disturbing sequence, Milly's pain and disappointment underlining our sense of the ugliness to which Kate's plot has brought both Merton and herself. The major source of disturbance is their moral deterioration, the collapse of all emotional fineness. What Kate is doing to Milly is scarcely worse than what she has done to herself, the coldness necessary to the execution of her scheme isolating her not only from Milly but from Merton, for whom she can no longer feel desire or even tenderness. As for Merton, this man of high principles is now reduced to forcing sex upon a woman who doesn't want it. Sexuality itself has been poisoned, along with the characters' capacity for spontaneity, intimacy and affection. The progress of the film is the charting of the effects of spiritual poison.

From the frantic, furtive sex act the film cuts to a tranquil long shot (but accompanied by quietly ominous music) of Milly's palazzo across a wide stretch of water; it is still night, the scene illuminated by a row of lights along the bank. This introduces a medium shot of Milly sitting up in bed, calm now but obviously puzzled and hurt. A tentative tap at the door. Kate, her matador jacket shed, her tie loose around her neck, appears in the doorway, contrite, anxious. Milly asks her 'Please don't lie to me,' then asks if she loves Merton. Kate hesitates, says 'No.' She looks genuinely regretful, and seems to be both lying and not lying: her commitment to Merton is as strong as ever, yet does she, at that moment, 'love' him? He has just forced her into a clumsy, uncomfortable and sordid back street copulation which she didn't desire, and she now seems too much a slave to her plot to 'love' anyone. The ambiguous lie, however, promptly entails a definite one: Milly asks 'Why did you leave?', and Kate tells her she had to talk to Merton alone 'to tell him I didn't love him'. Milly is silent, troubled, uncertain; Kate continues, telling her that she's decided to return to London tomorrow. Milly asks 'Because of me?' Kate: 'Because of you. Because of Merton. And because of me. I'm in your way.' When Milly tells her not to be 'ridiculous' and says she will be sorry if Kate goes, Kate sadly, ironically, repeats Milly's earlier 'Please don't lie to me,' ending with the faintest hint of a smile, then adds 'I don't want you to hate me,' responding to Milly's denial with 'Yes, you will. If I stay, you will.'

'Don't look at me like that. You've thought the same things.' 'You want me to seduce a dying girl.'

This is another of Bonham Carter's finest moments, in a performance containing so many fine ones. The ambiguity – Milly will hate her (a) if she comes between her and Merton or (b) if she learns the truth – is clearly deliberate, but Kate's face also tells us that it expresses something deeper than a private irony, the ambiguity of Kate's own feelings. She *doesn't* want Milly to hate her – a part of her, resurfacing in the wake of a disturbing night, genuinely still wants Milly's happiness and affection. Yet she can't relinquish her scheme, because it obsesses her but also because to abandon it would involve confessing to Milly and admitting to her own relationship with Merton. She also can't trust herself not to allow jealousy to overcome her again if she has to be a spectator to Merton's courtship of Milly. This is film acting at its subtlest, conveying in the slightest flickers of expression and intonation what it has taken me half a page to describe. Bonham Carter does not merely act Kate, she inhabits her.

It is morning. Merton arrives to find Milly, alone, at breakfast in the little enclosed courtyard of the palazzo. She tells him of Kate's departure, and on 'She decided last night' pauses, looks at him across the table, chin slightly thrust out, a look of challenge. His reaction to the news will tell her where they stand. Merton has of course committed himself to Kate's project, her reward for allowing him to consummate their relationship. When Milly tells him she hopes he won't be leaving also, he replies 'No. I like it here.' But he can't continue to meet her eyes. The little scene, introducing the film's next 'movement', returns us to a precarious harmony (the perfectly symmetrical composition, centred on the small breakfast table, sunlight, a new day) signifying a fresh start after the previous night's disturbance, Milly now happily accepting her freedom to pursue a relationship with Merton.

The feeling of renewal is developed through the following scene: a brilliantly clear, fresh day, Milly and Merton walking together, first through a boat-building and repair yard, where they argue about the 'prow' and 'stern' of the gondolas and where Milly rediscovers a youthfulness and ebullience from her delight in Merton's company. The walk continues through the tourist's Venice of monuments, churches, open spaces, ancient bridges, St Mark's. Milly takes delight in everything she sees, Merton tells her his exaggeratedly provocative wish to see it all razed to build houses for the poor. Milly indignantly accuses him of unfairly using an 'emotional argument' with which she couldn't possibly disagree, Merton telling her to admit she's lost, the exchange collapsing in laughter and playful physical contact, Milly poking him in the chest, Merton touching her cheek with an affection that clearly isn't feigned. Then, abruptly, night and a storm, the tightly framed two-shot of the couple giving place to a panoramic view of the city under a dark sky lit by lightning flashes, then a series of shots of rain-drenched streets and buildings.

This introduces two short wordless scenes, first Merton alone, then Kate, each looking troubled and unhappy, suggestive of some form of vaguely telepathic communication. Merton, we assume, even aside from his guilt feelings, has been shaken by his suddenly finding Milly attractive – we see him looking out from behind bars, as if from a prison. Direct cut from him in close-up to Kate in medium long shot, the shots linked by the rain streaming down the window behind her. Kate's room is unidentified, but it lacks the gaudy opulence of Aunt Maud's Lancaster Gate mansion and we assume she has taken lodgings. She stands looking out at the rain, her arms folded, her expression suggesting profound disturbance, her doubts of Merton overwhelming her plans.

The downpour in Venice continues. As Merton fails to visit Milly, Milly (against Susan's advice and concern for her) goes to Merton. He is packing, the suitcase open on his bed as Milly stands in the doorway. She gives no sign she's noticed, but, as he uses the rain as an excuse for not visiting, pointedly comments that it 'hasn't stopped for three days'. Abrupt change of scene to a restaurant at night; they are toasting each other with glasses of a colourless, flaming spirit (sambucca perhaps?). She asks what he's been doing ('Pacing the room. Drawing on the window') and when she challenges him ('Packing your bags?') pauses, thinks, then tells her 'And unpacking them.' She asks 'Why did you stay? Really?', and he replies, again after a pause, 'I have nothing to go back to.' Throughout this dialogue he sounds like an actor speaking lines from a play he's learnt. When she suggests 'Your work?' his response is 'Oh, I don't believe in any of the things I write about. I fake passion. I fake conviction,' a response that seems to falsify the character as he has been presented hitherto. Has his involvement in a highly suspect and mercenary plot already destroyed his idealism? And if he is lying, what is the lie supposed to gain? Is he simply trying to show Milly that he really has no reason to leave, or (his idealism being his most obvious asset) does he want, on some level, to alienate her? I think myself that with Merton the film loses at times its usually sharp focus, its precision of insight into motivation, reaction and perception.

The most obvious explanation is that something was needed here to provoke Milly's immediate response, which is of great importance, both to her own characterisation and to what follows. She tells him that *she* believes in him: 'I have a good feeling. I think everything's going to happen for you, Merton – sooner than you think… With certain people, I *know.*' She immediately has a coughing fit but blames it on the alcohol ('I was trying to impress you'), following this immediately with 'I'm going to make a fool of myself tonight.'

Elliott here is at her most irresistible, yet coming from any other character the speech would be highly dubious. Clearly she is not simply trusting her instincts (that Merton is cut out for great things) – she knows (and he is supposed not to) that the 'everything' that's 'going to happen' for Merton will happen because she intends to seduce him (which, as later events confirm, is precisely what she means by 'making a fool of' herself), and that she will then die ('…sooner than you think') and leave him all her money. But if she is trying to buy him (her money will be available whether she dies or not), as Maggie Verver in *The Golden Bowl* buys herself a European prince, she is quite innocent of anything shameful – it is an impulse of pure generosity and love. Few actresses, surely, could carry this off convincingly.

The following sequences intercut Milly's determined seduction of Merton with Kate's letter to him expressing her fears. Milly, winning an argument, strikes a bargain: Merton may walk her home on condition that she walk him home first. Their walk to Merton's lodgings, Milly hanging on to his arm, happily giggling, provokes Merton's comment 'You're drunk, aren't you?' (which precisely echoes his line to Kate during the gondola ride, here shorn of its hostility and no longer a reprimand), answered by Milly's 'Not as drunk as I'm pretending to be' (this 'innocent' young girl knows exactly what she's about, and admits it with disarming frankness). Cut to Kate, a close-up mirror shot, her letter delivered as internal monologue as she confronts her reflection, judging, frightened, but not turning away. Her face is deathly pale, the round mirror frames her, enclosing her, turning her into a pallid image of her former self; one hand is bent under her chin, the other clasping the letter. Her voiceover continues over the couple's walk, as she speaks of 'following [them] along the streets and canals. Sometimes I see you touch her' (they are arm in arm). They arrive at Merton's lodging, he tells her that now he must take *her* home, but she says that 'We have to go all the way inside,' a sentence within which the phrase 'go all the way' carries its clear meaning. She adds 'I told you I was going to make a fool of myself,' and he tells her, gently but firmly, 'I don't want you to.' This exactly defines Merton's current position – he has come to care very much for Milly as a person, but doesn't want a sexual relationship, partly because of his commitment to Kate, partly because he has never found Milly sexually attractive. Elliott beautifully conveys Milly's reaction – disappointed, but touched by his gentleness and solicitude (whether she sees this as moral scruple, a reluctance to take advantage of a woman who's somewhat drunk, or because he hasn't yet quite got over Kate and her apparently decisive abandonment of him). We are returned to Kate before her mirror, now looking down, begging Merton, even if he doesn't answer it, to 'Read this letter again …and again. And every time she looks at you' – she looks up, meeting her own eyes again, as if she were imitating Milly looking at Merton, replacing her – 'every time she smiles, don't forget I love you more.' We may doubt, I think, that Kate loves him 'more'. Certainly she loves him quite differently (as everyone seems to be asking nowadays, what *is* love anyway?). Both women need him, but in different ways, Kate out of a kind of desperation that has its roots in her deprived and wretched background, Milly because she wants to 'live' before she dies. Neither love, then, is exactly selfless. Yet Milly has shown a certain faith in him, and seems to respond to his idealism, while Kate (in the scene in the newspaper office) showed no real interest in Merton's work whatever, telling him of his article merely that it sounds 'angry'.

The water at night, buoys moving slightly, a suggestion of uneasiness. Then rain. Merton and Milly enter a church for shelter, the church in the process of restoration, scaffolding rising up to the ceiling. Milly is absurdly angry because no one is working (in the middle of the night!) – 'How can they restore it if no one's working?' – her repressed frustration expressing itself in displacement. He tells her that she can 'always come and see it another time, it won't go away'. She looks at him, he turns away, suddenly understanding. Milly climbs the scaffolding, recapitulating her climb up to the parapet of St Mark's – but this time Merton follows. At the top is a 'private' space, behind two flimsy curtains. She kisses him, her eyes pleading; his arm, at first held stiff and awkward at his side, moves around her. We are shown his face, his uneasy response, accepting her embrace but looking over her shoulder, almost into camera, troubled. Then he returns her kiss. The film cuts there, but the implication that they make love is clear from the acting.

Next morning, rain continuing. Merton is standing at his window (echoing Kate in London). Then he sits down at his desk to write a letter: 'My dearest Kate, Everything I have done, I've done for you. Only it gets harder every day. She's *alive*, Kate. More alive than anyone I've ever known.' We hear the last words in voiceover as (we presume as a direct reaction to the letter) Kate arrives, and is welcomed, at Lord Mark's: 'My dear Kate. Such a pleasure.' Her face is drawn, troubled, guilty. 'What could be so urgent?' Two short, strongly contrasted scenes in Venice follow. First, dense mist, slow track right followed by static camera: Merton in a gondola, turned away by Eugenio (Milly is 'fatigued'); second, the Piazza, pouring rain, a rapid track right as waiters rush to upturn chairs on the outdoor tables, atmosphere of panic. Merton, sheltering, hurrying past, glimpses Lord Mark reading a newspaper at a table in Florian's. He goes back to check: the place has been vacated, the newspaper is lying on the table, a waiter is removing glasses. A further, more insistent, more frantic confrontation with Eugenio: 'Miss Theale wants to see no one. Very tired.' But he admits, implicitly, to Lord Mark's visit.

Merton insists 'Tell Miss Theale I came to see her. Tell her.'

Even Eugenio (Georgio Serafini), who has probably no more than a minute of screen time, is a vivid little cameo: the 'perfect' servant of the rich, devoted while extremely impressed by money, looking down on obviously 'inferior' people like Merton (from whom little could be extracted).

This sequence of brief, barely sketched scenes, the brevity suggesting speed and inexorability, drive the film towards its climax. 'A lady' has come to visit Merton, announced by the old woman who runs his lodging-house. But it isn't Milly. Merton and Susan are shown to a table in the little eating area for an uncomfortable talk, the old woman bringing a lamp to the table, which Merton rejects – he prefers not to be in too much illumination. His question (after 'Is she sick?'): 'Is she dying?' Susan's response is simply 'Did you know?' – which Merton can't answer, although his face confesses. He asks 'Will she see me?' Susan says she thinks so, then tells him earnestly, 'Tell her it isn't true.' Merton still stalls, so she spells it out: 'That you've been with Kate. All the time…From the beginning.' As Merton sits down he seems tightly enclosed by a black frame – the dark walls on either side of the stained glass window before which he was standing. He still doesn't answer Susan's question explicitly, but again the truth is implicitly acknowledged – he deflects his anger at himself on to Lord Mark: 'Did he want to hurt her? Did he want to *kill* her?' But as he says it he immediately falls silent, as his own sense of guilt overcomes him: he and Kate haven't killed Milly (she was dying anyway), but they have clearly, between them, hastened her death and destroyed the illusion of happiness that they had also, between them, constructed. Susan says 'Kate must have told him,' which he refuses to believe until she adds, for the first time accusingly, judgmentally, 'Who else knew?'

She brings Merton to Milly's room, initiating the film's most painful, and most touching scene (which has no equivalent in the novel, in which Merton returns to London without seeing Milly again). They stand for a moment in the doorway, and we see Milly from their point of view.

The poignance of her descent (almost a plunge, as if she didn't wish to live any longer) into death is intensified by the splendour of her surroundings, what money *can* buy juxtaposed with what it can't: in long shot, she is lying on an ornate white sofa, behind her a vast classical painting (we can't make out of what, the point being the opulence). In a decor dominated by pale gold (the chair upholstery) Milly is wearing a simple white satin slip, and her face is paler than we have previously seen it, the whiteness and pallor thrown into relief by her luxuriant red hair, suggestive of energy and vitality. If the film has at times glossed over awkward moments (especially, moments concerning Merton), here it is unflinching in sparing the viewer (and Merton) nothing. Not that it ever loses its emotional poise: this is a scene in which a lapse into hysteria and melodramatics – or into sentimentality – would be disastrous.

Parenthetically, I want to say here that one of the greatest problems I have encountered in writing this monograph is that the film's greatness – supported certainly by a marvellous screenplay – is ultimately dependent upon its actors, and great acting (as finer minds than mine have already discovered) cannot be adequately described in words. Even several pages of frame enlargements from a single scene would not offer more than an approximation, as the essence of acting is movement – the movement of the lips or of an eyebrow, the flicker of an expression that changes constantly – rather than a frozen moment. One can offer only some crude approximation of the effect, and then say 'Look for yourself.' That, then, is what I shall say here, instead of trying to descibe what Alison Elliott (for,

'I can't fool myself forever.'

'He came here to hurt me and brought me a box of biscuits.' 'Don't. We're beyond that, you and I.' Merton's reaction.

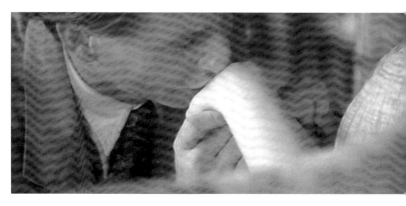

'I love you … Both of you.' 'I'm so sorry.'

excellent as Linus Roache consistently is, the scene belongs to her) conveys in the continuously shifting expressions of her features: look, please.

The scene breaks down into three stages. First Merton's attempt to resume the relationship at the point it had reached, no longer to please Kate but to make Milly happy, restore her self-esteem, and in doing so assuage his own guilt. Second his assertion, and Milly's rejection, of the falsehood of Lord Mark's revelations. Third Merton's collapse and plea for forgiveness. The first stage culminates in Milly's 'Do I look like I could climb a church scaffold?' (in response to Merton's promise of 'the same things we did before'), followed by her frank, unself-pitying acknowledgment that 'I can't fool myself forever.' This precipitates Merton's 'It isn't true, Milly...What Lord Mark told you,' and her painful attempt (for his sake?) to sidestep the issue – to avoid directly confronting him with the fact that he is still lying to her and that she knows it – by

'And I said, O that I had wings like a dove, for then I would fly away, and be at rest.' 'I was scared of losing you.'

producing Lord Mark's ridiculous gift. On the lid is Ophelia drowning, which Lord Mark hadn't noticed when he presented it to her ('He never does anything quite right. He came here to hurt me and he brought me a box of biscuits'). When Merton persists ('Milly. What could I do to persuade you?') she at last reveals the depth of the hurt, her face unlike we've seen before ('Don't. We're beyond that, you and I'), then utters one of the most heartbreaking lines in cinema: 'I love you. *Both* of you.' Again I must ask, how many actresses could get away with that line? – it could so easily emerge as sickeningly sentimental. Suffice it to say that, as surely as Helena Bonham Carter inhabits Kate, Alison Elliott inhabits Milly: the line, with its transcendent tenderness and forgiveness, has not the slightest sense of self-conscious posturing. It provokes Merton's (and my own, every time) collapse into tears – tears not only for Milly, but for Kate and himself.

The camera cuts to long shot, then tracks slowly back from our last view of Milly, Merton kneeling beside the sofa, his head in her arms as he weeps. Cut to Merton sitting alone at a table outside a nearby cafe by a bridge. Susan, at first a tiny speck, crosses the bridge towards him. She is dressed from head to foot in black. There is no need for words.

There follows Milly's funeral, the gondola bearing the coffin crossing the water to a mausoleum (the image, in long shot, for a moment evokes Böcklin's *Isle of the Dead*). Then Merton, in voiceover, delivers (to himself, as internal monologue) the brief oration: 'My heart is sore pained within me, and the terrors of death have fallen upon me. Fearfulness and trembling have come upon me, and a horror has overwhelmed me. And I said, Oh that I had wings like a dove, for then I would fly away, and be at rest.' In James's novel it is Milly who is characterised (at several points) as a dove. Here, in one of Hossein Amini's most audacious departures, the speech clearly refers primarily to Merton himself.

And so, the final scene (or what *should* have been the final scene). London, night, rain. A cab draws up outside Merton's apartment building. Kate, in black, gets out and mounts the steps. Cut to Merton in his cramped and dingy living-room, sitting over a small coal fire, brooding, chin in hands. At Kate's knock and subsequent call he barely moves.

Then, when she knocks again, after some hesitation he reluctantly rises and slowly goes to the door: instead of a joyous lovers' reunion, it is an ordeal he knows he must go through. He tells Kate he was 'next door' (has lying become habitual and automatic or does he simply want to get it over as quickly and painlessly as possible? This is the woman with whom he is supposed to be passionately in love). In answer to Kate's question he admits (frankly now) that he has been back about a fortnight, adding by way of excuse, but sarcastically, that he 'couldn't rush to' her, he was 'keeping to our wonderful system' – the system, presumably, of pretending to love Milly, the sarcasm implying that Kate *only* pretended. She responds, quietly yet firmly, 'She was my friend too,' which unleashes more extreme sarcasm ('Of course she was. Our great friend. The three of us so…'). She cuts him short ('Stop it'). He charges her that she knew Lord Mark would go straight to Milly, adding 'And what about all your plans?' Kate tells him, simply and honestly, 'I was scared of losing you.' Still very pale under her black veil, she looks painfully vulnerable, all her earlier self-confidence and strength evaporated. She goes to him, touching his cheek as he sits at his desk; he moves his face away, then briefly relents, takes her hand, brushing it with his lips. But he immediately turns aside to give her an envelope from his desk: 'This is for you.'

But it's addressed to Merton and he hasn't opened it. Both know what it contains, but Kate spells it out: 'She's made you rich.' He tells Kate to take it, adding brutally 'It's your prize.' She carries the letter to the fire and lays it on the glowing coals. As Kate herself says later, Merton

Milly's testament.

will still get the money ('Burning a letter doesn't change that'), but
Bonham Carter makes it clear that it is more than an empty melodramatic
gesture: she is telling Merton that the money is no longer the question, it
is her symbolic act of contrition and renunciation. In revealing the facts to
Lord Mark she has already made it clear that without Merton the money
would be meaningless to her.

   Kate moves into the dark bedroom, sits on the bed, begins to
undress. Her body is hunched over, long shot emphasising her slightness,
the essential fragility beneath the toughness she had developed to cope
with the squalid realities of her existence; the act of taking off one's
clothes has never looked so awkward. Naked, she leans back on her
hands, offering herself, but without desire or the expectation of pleasure.
When she lies on her side, turned away, he tells her 'I'm going to write to
her lawyers,' to which, turning her head to face him, she says quietly, 'You

'I know what it says. She's made you rich.' 'Take it. It's your prize.'

want me to persuade you to keep her money. Is that what you want?' She is wrong again, of course – Kate never fully understands Merton, she has grown up in an environment in which idealism would be a superfluous luxury. He tells her he'll 'never take her money', and she raises herself to put her arms around his neck and draw him to her. Sitting on the bed holding each other they rock gently a moment; Kate looks over his shoulder at the drab dark room, the rain falling outside. Then she helps him undress. Naked, he lies down on his back, completely passive (in complete contrast to his 'masculine' sexual aggressiveness in Venice), and whispers, barely audibly, 'I love you Kate,' but the words, totally passionless, sound as if he's trying to convince himself. She lies on top of him, then gives the inevitable response 'I love you too,' but it comes across as more frightened than convincing, as if she was no longer certain of its reality. The suggestion is that love between them (presented in the early part of the film as fully authentic) is no longer possible: they will never again be able to look at each other without arousing the sense of their shared guilt. Merton's alienation is so plain that Kate, lying in his arms, is driven to ask 'What are you thinking about?', adding, accusingly, when he doesn't answer, 'You're still in love with her.' Merton: 'I was never in love with her.' We register this, I think, as true: he learnt to love Milly, just as Kate had once loved her, before the hardening of her plan into action (you can't afford to love someone you propose to victimise), but he was never 'in love' with her. Kate, perceptively, elaborates: 'While she was alive, no.' He is silent a moment, then implicitly concurs ('I'm sorry, Kate. I'm so sorry'), to which Kate replies, more automatic than sincere, 'It doesn't matter.' They cling to each other in a kind of forced passion, and he tells her 'She wanted us to be together.' Kate then attempts copulation, with a man who cannot be aroused. As she abandons it, Softley cuts to a desolate long shot, Kate turning aside and collapsing in despair, the bars at the bottom of the bed shutting the viewer out from any possible further intimacy.

The laserdisc cover prominently quotes a reviewer on CBS-TV as summing the film up as 'Satisfying, Sexy, Superb'. Aside from the annoyingly slick alliteration I have no quarrel with the last of these terms; I would qualify 'satisfying' with 'almost'. But 'sexy' requires more drastic qualification. The film *is* 'sexy' (I suppose) in that, chiefly through Milly, it celebrates a completely open, healthy and generous sexuality, by no means limited to specifically sexual activity but generating the aliveness (in Merton's words she's 'more alive than anyone I've ever known') that gives this dying woman her attractiveness and fascination. The two explicit sex scenes between Kate and Merton, on the other hand, are quite the reverse of 'sexy', disturbing in their coldness and alienation, the final scene singularly *un*satisfying (which is its point) in the absence of consummation.

The scene culminates in a final attempt, despite the failure of sexual intimacy, at some kind of reconciliation. As they lie, physically close but totally separate, Merton reiterates that he intends to reject Milly's money. Kate tells him to do whatever he wants, and he responds 'I want to marry *you*, Kate. Without her money.' But if that is his condition, she has one too: he must promise her, on his word of honour, that he is not in love with Milly's memory. He can't answer. After a moment Kate gets up, and we hear her dressing. The camera remains on Merton's face, moving in to full-screen close-up as he recalls (and we see) two moments of the nocturnal gondola ride: Milly's face in close-up as she lies back against the cushions, then the exchange between Milly and Kate ('Come closer…'), as the boats come together in the narrow passage. The first of these is a false memory, quite different from its original (there, Milly's face expressed a fusion of conflicting feelings, yearning, delight, regret; here, its expression is simply happy); in the second, Softley reverses the original editing – there, cutting from distant long shot to closer, here cutting back from closer to distant – as if the moment remembered were receding from any possible realisation. In the first, Merton is sentimentalising Milly, reducing her to a happy face. The second is especially interesting, as it records a moment in the *women's* intimacy and the possibility of a harmonious three-way relationship, which Merton previously rejected but is now nostalgically remembering.

The film returns us to his troubled face, and I still think that is where it should have left us: I continue to resent the last two shots. However, repeated viewings have made them seem rather more obscure and ambiguous than I gave them credit for. It seems possible to read them as *Merton's* collapse into sentimentality rather than the film's – his own personal evasion of guilt by indulging a morbid fantasy, anticipated by the false memory-shot of Milly. And then the practical question arises: how is he going to *live* in Venice? He has presumably jettisoned his newspaper job. This leads to another possible reading (totally contradicted by the tone of the little scene and its accompanying music): he has, after all, accepted Milly's money and has come to settle in her palazzo. I don't take this reading seriously, but the film lays itself open to it. What exactly Amini and Softley (if they were responsible) intended here seems very unclear and unfocused; the shots in any case confirm that the film's weak spot is Merton. The chief objection to the last two shots remains: they appear to redeem Merton while simply abandoning Kate, and Kate remains the film's tragic heroine, its most complex character, and its ultimate victim – the victim of her background, of all the pressures on her, of a society constructed and conducted on monetary values.

I shall close by returning briefly to the question of adaptation. I mentioned earlier that the Kate/Merton dénouement is the closest scene in the film to James, and the assertion needs some development as the differences remain so great. It corresponds to James's closing scene in its position in the novel, its location, and its outcome. That said, the differences go far beyond the fact that the characters in the film take off their clothes and attempt copulation. In the novel, Merton offers to pass the money on to Kate if she won't accept his condition, and it remains ambiguous whether or not she will accept it. She has done nothing to renounce it previously: in the novel she was not jealous of Milly, she did not set up Lord Mark to intervene. The film, however, leaves us in no doubt that, when forced to a choice, Kate chooses the relationship over the money – only to find that she has lost both. Helena Bonham Carter's Kate is closer to James's conception than the film's Merton and Milly are to their originals, but there is still a great difference: James's Kate is more mature, more secure, and although she is only twenty-three she strikes me more as a young Sigourney Weaver. Bonham Carter, as well as seeming very young, brings a nervous vulnerability to the role that ultimately makes her scarcely more James's Kate than Alison Elliott is James's Milly. In fact the casting of the leads and the changes from the novel seem to go so intimately together that one may well wonder which was chicken and which was egg: was the screenplay completed as we have it, or were changes made after Bonham Carter and Elliott were cast?

However detailed, a written account of a work of art can never replace it. For one thing, in writing this I have become increasingly aware of the critic's helplessness: so much of the film's excellence cannot be expressed in words; for another, first-hand experience may well show that much in the interpretation I have attempted is open to argument. What I have above all wished to do is share the intense pleasure I have derived from what I would finally describe as a flawed masterpiece.

Credits

The Wings of the Dove

USA/UK 1997

Director
Iain Softley
Producers
Stephan Evans, David Parfitt
Screenplay
Hossein Amini
Based on the novel by Henry James
Director of Photography
Eduardo Serra
Editor
Tariq Anwar
Production Designer
John Beard
Music/Music Conductor
Edward Shearmur

©Miramax Films &
Renaissance Dove Ltd
Production Companies
Miramax Films presents
a Renaissance Films
production
an Iain Softley film
Executive Producers
Bob Weinstein, Harvey
Weinstein, Paul Feldsher
Line Producer
Mark Cooper
Associate Producer
Caroline Wood
Production Co-ordinator
Erica Bensly
Venice Crew Production Manager
Rosanna Roditi

Unit Managers
Christian McWilliams
Venice Crew:
David Ambrosi
Location Managers
Chris Wheeldon
Venice Crew:
Dominique De Langes
Assistant Location Manager
Dee Gregson
Financial Controller
Liz Barron
Assistant/Post-production Accountant
Margaret Teatum
Assistant Accountant
Diane Pontefract
Fiscal Representative
Venice Crew:
Enzo Sisti
Accountant
Venice Crew:
Carla Zacchia Legali
Payroll Clerk
Venice Crew:
Marilena La Ferrara
Cashier
Venice Crew:
Maurizio Graziosi
Producer's Assistant
Cleone Clarke
Executive Producer's Assistant
Jennifer McAlear
Production Secretary
Kay Robinson

Production Assistants
Stephanie Avery
Venice Crew:
Fabio Vianello, Fabio
Bozzetti, Anita Tomaselli
Production Runner
Caroline Moore
Floor Runners
Ben Burt
Venice Crew:
Donata Cecconi, Luciano
Tito
Runner/Driver
Natasha Dack
2nd Unit Director
Venice:
Gala Wright
1st Assistant Director
Simon Moseley
2nd Assistant Directors
Richard Styles
2nd Unit UK:
Guy Heeley
Venice Crew:
Luca Lacchin
3rd Assistant Directors
Barbara Mulcahy
2nd Unit UK:
Rebecca Tucker
2nd Unit UK Additional:
Avshalom Pollak
Venice Crew:
Sergio Ghetti, Pierantonio
Novara, Giovanni Silvestrini
Director's Assistant
Gala Wright
Script Supervisor
Anna Worley

Casting
Michelle Guish
US:
Billy Hopkins, Suzanne
Smith, Kerry Barden
Extras:
Ray Knight Casting
2nd Unit Venice Extras
Director:
Daniela Foà
Crowd Marshall
2nd Unit Venice:
Nicola Minghetti
Camera Operators
Mike Proudfoot
2nd Unit UK:
Nick Schlesinger
2nd Unit Venice:
Pascal Ridao
Steadicam Operators
Venice Crew:
Alessandro Bolognesi
2nd Unit UK:
Peter Robertson
Focus Pullers
Dave Morgan
2nd Unit UK:
Brad Larner
2nd Unit Venice:
Thierry Pouget
Clapper Loaders
John Ferguson
2nd Unit UK:
John Gamble
2nd Unit Venice:
Miles Proudfoot
Key Grip
2nd Unit Venice:
Stefano Biscaro
Grips
Tony Turner
2nd Unit Venice:
Werner Bacciu, Nicola
Bruso, Paolo Frasson

Grip Rigger
2nd Unit Venice:
Regis Benedettelli
Labourer Grips
2nd Unit Venice:
Raffaele Scarpa, Marco
Alzetta
Camera Trainee
Andrew Gleboff
Video Operator
Roger Sharland
Video Assist
2nd Unit Venice:
Emanuele Leurini
Crane Operator
Andy Hopkins
Gaffers
Steve Costello
2nd Unit Venice:
Dario Gardi
Best Boy
Roy Branch
Electricians
Tony Burns, Steve Casey,
Andy Taylor
2nd Unit Venice:
Cristiano Giavedoni, Angelo
Russo
**Electrician/Genny
Operator**
Rob Brock
Practical Electrician
George Vince
Labourer Electricians
2nd Unit Venice:
Daniel Bacciu, Luca
Casagrande, Tommaso
Dabala
Genny Operators
2nd Unit Venice:
Michele Turchetto, Andrea
Castellan
Stills
Mark Tillie

Digital Visual Effects
The Film Factory at VTR
London
Special Effects
Effects Associates
Senior Technician:
Dominic Tuohy
Technician:
Steve Warner
Graphics Supervisor
Danny Walker
Associate Editor
Liz Green
Assistant Editors
Saska Simpson, Jay
Coquillon, Katya Jezzard
Editor's Runner
Mickey McKnight
Supervising Art Director
Andrew Sanders
Art Directors
Martyn John
Venice Crew:
Andrea Faini
Assistant Art Directors
Ray Chan
Venice Crew:
Francesca Fezzi, Ornella
Baraldo
Art Department Assistant
Caireen Todd
Set Decorator
Joanne Woollard
Assistant Set Decorator
Eliza Solesbury
Assistant Set Dressers
Venice Crew:
Alvise Grandese, Franco
Contini, Pietro Tessera
Draughtsmen
Gary Freeman, Rod McLean
Storyboard Artist
Jane Clark

Art Department Runner
Claire Richards
Construction Managers
Peter Verard
2nd Unit Venice:
Roberto Laurenzi
Construction Co-ordinator
Dave Middleton
Supervising Carpenters
Steve Allaway, Richard
Weames
Carpenters
David Abbott, Tony Allaway,
Joe Alley, Lee Apsey, Warren
Browne, Dave Bubb,
Anthony Challenor, Peter
Duffey, Dave Edwards,
Eddie Farrell, Garry Fisher,
Frank Gill, Peter Grove, Kevin
Hedges, Frank Henry, Bryce
Johnstone, Bill Lyons, Harry
Portlock, Ronnie Ross, Paul
Sansom, Kenneth Small,
Gary Stopps, Graham
Weames, David Wells
2nd Unit Venice:
Paolo Pugglotto, Vito Reina,
Alessandro Anselmi, Pietro
Petri
Wood Machinist
Karl George
Supervising Painter
Alan Grenham
Scenic Painters
Stephen Marquiss, Anthony
Rhone, Steven Sibley
Painters
Ernie Bell, Frank Berlin,
Warren Grenham, David
Haynes, Arthur Healy,
Edward McLaren, Brian
Shelley, Lee Shelley,
Kenneth Welland, Brian
Western

2nd Unit Venice:
Paola Saraval, Elisabetta
Frazuoli, Riccardo Andreotti
Supervising Rigger
Bill Beenham
Riggers
Gary Dormer, Bill Howe, Iain
Lowe, Ian Norgate, Kenny
Richards
Chargehand Stagehand
Clive Rivers
Stagehands
Stuart Davidson, Jeremiah
Delaney, Clifford Rashbrock,
Eddie O'Neill
Trainee Stagehand
Danny Delaney
Standby Carpenters
David Coley, Dave Creed
Standby Painter
Robin Heinson
Standby Riggers
Simon Alderton, Steve
Challis
Standby Stagehand
David Jones
Labourers
2nd Unit Venice:
Marino Ingrassia, Giacomo
Brasolin, Paolo Fortunati,
Giulio Ravenna, Alberto
Tomasini, Luca Massarotto,
Klaus Bittner, David Bittner,
Paul Bittner, Italo Gerardi
Property Buyers
Belinda Edwards
Venice Crew:
Giorgio Pansini
Property Master
Barry Gibbs
Propmen
Venice Crew:
Floriano Porzionato, Stefano
Calcaterra

Property Storemen
Darryl Paterson, Peter
Bryant, Paul Turley
Dressing Props
Laurence Wells, Terry Wells
Jr, Lee Bryant
Standby Propmen
Barry Arnold, Bill Hargreaves
Costume Designers
Sandy Powell
Associate:
Frank Gardiner
Costume Supervisor
Clare Spragge
Wardrobe Mistress
Jacki Thomas
Wardrobe Master
Anthony Brookman
Costume Assistants
Jenny Hawkins, Vanessa
Munro, Nicola Ball
Wardrobe Assistants
2nd Unit Venice:
Shizu Omachi, Ermelinda
Scilinguo
Costume Makers
Cecilia Burrows, Claire
Christie, Yvonne Jackson-
French, Janette Haslem,
Charles Lester, Patricia
Lester, Peter Lewis, Anne
Nichols, Alison O'Brien,
Hilary Parkinson, Suzanne
Parkinson, Gwen Russell,
Carmen Verttoretti
2nd Unit Venice:
Alba Alzetta, Cristiano
Galzerano, Anna Maria
Genvise, Loredana Malusa,
Luca Critofoli
Millinery
Sean Barrett
Fabric Painting/Dyeing
John Cowell

Shoe Makers
Pompeii Footwear
Costume Suppliers
Angels and Bermans,
Cosprop, Nicolao Atelier
Chief Make-up Artist
Sallie Jaye
Make-up Artists
Kerin Parfitt, Darren Phillips
Make-up Assistants
2nd Unit Venice 1st:
Cristiana Bertini
2nd Unit Venice 2nd:
Laura Borzelli
Chief Hairdresser
Jan Archibald
Supervising Hairdresser
Venice:
Jeanette Freeman
Hairdressers
Astrid Schikorra, Anita
Burger
Assistant Hairdressers
2nd Unit Venice 1st:
Carla Ruffert
2nd Unit Venice 2nd:
Elide Velicogna
Titles Design
Shaun Webb, Graphic
Design
Main Title/Film Opticals
Peter Govey Opticals
Grader
Michael Stainer
Music Performed by
The London Metropolitan
Orchestra
Additional Orchestrations
John Bell
Music Supervision
Maggie Rodford, Becky
Bentham, Air Edel
Associates Limited

Music Editors
Tim Handley, Dashiell Rae
Music Engineer
Steve McLaughlin
Assistant Music Engineer
David Walter
Musicians' Contractor
Andy Brown
Copyist
Vic Fraser
Choreographer
Stuart Hopps
**Production Sound
Recordist**
Peter Lindsay
Sound Consultant
Eddie Joseph
Re-recording Mixers
Robin O'Donoghue,
Dominic Lester, Dean
Humphries
Sound Editors
Martin Evans, Matt Grime,
Nick Lowe, Nigel Mills, Mike
Wood
Assistant Sound Editors
Gordon Greenaway, Andrea
Issac, Dan Laurie
ADR Editor
Steven Schwalbe
Foley Artistes
Paula Boram, Lauren Potter
Foley Mixer
Edward Colyer
Foley Editor
Stan Fiferman
Assistant Foley Editor
Geoff R. Brown
**Sound Maintenance
Engineer**
Malcolm Rose
Sound Assistant
Stephen Finn

Sound Trainee
Sam Kruger
Neg Cutter
Mike Fraser
Horse Co-ordinator
Debbie Kaye
Boat Marshall
Venice Crew:
Maria Grazia Dabala
Veteran Vehicles
John Geary at Motorhouse
Etiquette Adviser
Cyril Dickman
Medical Adviser
Ron Stenner
Health and Safety Adviser
Brian Shemmings
Movement Consultant
Jane Gibson
Computers Supplied by
Infinite Loop Inc
Transport Manager
Tony Bird at Aeroshoot Film
Services
Unit Drivers
Mike Crawley, Terry English,
Mark Richards, Simon
Saunders, Phil Knight, Ron
Nanson
Camera Driver
Rob Fowle
Wardrobe Driver
Charlie Simpson
Make-up Driver
Kieran Smith
Props Standby Driver
John Botton
Dining Bus Driver
Ron Lowe
Dressing Props Driver
Doug Langston
Construction Driver
Bill Clare

Minibus Drivers
Howard Doubtfire, Phil
Edwards
Craft Services
2nd Unit Venice:
Carlo Forcellini, Lorenzo
Bellini, Ermanno Kerstich
Security
2nd Unit Venice:
Giorgio Scasso, Aldo
Mingardi
Caterers
2nd Unit UK:
Reel Food for Reel People,
Crew to Crew
Unit Nurses
2nd Unit UK:
Valerie Dyer, Marianne Lytton
2nd Unit Venice:
Giorgio Rossi, Mario De Poli
Stand-ins
Roy Beck, Clair Chrysler,
Joan Field, Lee Field, Maxine
Weavers
Unit Publicists
Sara Keene, Vikki Luya,
Corbett & Keene Ltd
EPK
The Special Treats
Production Company Ltd

Helena Bonham Carter
Kate Croy
Linus Roache
Merton Densher
Alison Elliott
Milly Theale
Elizabeth McGovern
Susan
Michael Gambon
Mr Croy, Kate's father
Alex Jennings
Lord Mark

Charlotte Rampling
Aunt Maud
Ben Miles
journalist 1
Philip Wright
journalist 2
Alexander John
butler
Shirley Chantrell
opium den lady
Diana Kent
Merton's party companion
Georgio Serafini
Eugenio
Rachaele Crisafulli
concierge

9,165 feet
101 minutes 50 seconds

Dolby digital
In Colour
Super 35

Filmed at
Shepperton Studios and on
location at Luton Hoo,
Knebworth House, The City
of London, Carlton House
Terrace, The National Liberal
Club, Kensington Gardens,
Syon House, Richmond
Fellowship, Brompton
Cemetery, Painshill Park,
Freemason's Hall, The Royal
Naval College Greenwich
and Venice, Italy

Credits compiled by
Markku Salmi,
BFI Filmographic Unit

Also Published

L'Argent
Kent Jones (1999)

Blade Runner
Scott Bukatman (1997)

Blue Velvet
Michael Atkinson (1997)

Caravaggio
Leo Bersani & Ulysse Dutoit (1999)

Crash
Iain Sinclair (1999)

The Crying Game
Jane Giles (1997)

Don't Look Now
Mark Sanderson (1996)

Easy Rider
Lee Hill (1996)

The Exorcist
Mark Kermode (1997, 2nd edn 1998)

Independence Day
Michael Rogin (1998)

Last Tango in Paris
David Thompson (1998)

Once Upon a Time in America
Adrian Martin (1998)

Seven
Richard Dyer (1999)

The Terminator
Sean French (1996)

The Thing
Anne Billson (1997)

The 'Three Colours' Trilogy
Geoff Andrew (1998)

The Right Stuff
Tom Charity (1997)

Women on the Verge of a Nervous Breakdown
Peter William Evans (1996)

WR – Mysteries of the Organism
Raymond Durgnat (1999)

Forthcoming

Dead Man
Jonathan Rosenbaum (2000)

Pulp Fiction
Dana Polan (2000)

Saló, or the Hundred and Twenty Days of Sodom
Gary Indiana (2000)

Thelma and Louise
Marita Sturken (2000)

Titanic
David M. Lubin (1999)